Scenes from Vicarage Life

Or

The Joy of Sexagesima

CATHERINE FOX

Catherine Fox

MONARCH
BOOKS

Oxford, UK, and Grand Rapids, Michigan, USA

First published by Monarch Books in the UK in 2001.
Reprinted in 2004 by Monarch Books
(a publishing imprint of Lion Hudson plc), Mayfield House,
256 Banbury Road, Oxford OX2 7DH
Tel: +44 (0) 1865 302750 Fax: +44 (0) 1865 302757.
Email: monarch@lionhudson.com
www.lionhudson.com

ISBN 1 85424 548 1 (UK)
ISBN 0 8254 6038 7 (USA)

Illustrations by Bridget Gillespie

Distributed by:
UK: STL, PO Box 300, Kingstown Broadway,
Carlisle, Cumbria CA3 0QS;
USA: Kregel Publications, PO Box 2607,
Grand Rapids, Michigan 49501.

Unless otherwise stated, Scripture quotations are
taken from the Holy Bible, New International Version,
copyright © 1973, 1978, 1984 by the International Bible Society,
Inclusive Language Version 1995, 1996.
Used by permission of Hodder and Stoughton Ltd.
All rights reserved.

British Library Cataloguing Data
A catalogue record for this book is available
from the British Library.

ACKNOWLEDGEMENTS

I would like to express my gratitude to the anonymous masses whose witticisims I have taken and passed off as my own. I would also like to thank my two sons for providing me with such good copy over the years. When you are older, boys, and want to kill me for making money out of the raw material of your lives, remember this – I bought you Pokemon cards and took you to Waterworld. You colluded. You can't expect that kind of luxury on a clergy stipend.

I would like to make a special mention of *The Church of England Newspaper*, and thank the staff for all their help and support. It was the deputy editor who first kindly invited me to write the weekly column in 1997. I took it on for a month and they haven't sacked me yet.

My thanks also go to the Friends of Clergy Spouses for their generous bequest which has kept me in gin and Janet Reger over the last year. Or would have done, if they'd had the foresight to exist.

Finally I would like to thank a vicar I know who has saved me from a number of errors in the writing of this book – and incorporated a few of his own (see Glossary) – and without whom happiness would not be possible again for a very long time.

*For the congregation at St Paul's
at the Crossing, Walsall,
with love*

CONTENTS

INTRODUCTION

This book is based on columns which first appeared in *The Church of England Newspaper*. I have tried to collect the material into helpful sections to make it as accessible as possible to the reader. Having come relatively late to Anglicanism, I am aware of how confusing it can be to outsiders—all the strange festivals, arcane language and funny clothes. I grew up in a denomination where S & M referred to Sankey and Moody's *Sacred Songs and Solos*, so you can imagine how big the culture shock has been. Even so, it is easy to forget what a strange world we inhabit here in the vicarage. We simultaneously operate in at least five separate timescales: the calendar year, the liturgical year, the tax year, the academic year and eternity.

In an attempt to make things less confusing I have decided to use the form of a Yearbook. Never before has useful information from three sources—*The Book of Common Prayer*, the *Alternative Service Book* and *Common Worship*—been so handily combined in one volume. I have also drawn on the great wealth available to us in the lives of the saints. Many of these great men and women of faith are sadly overlooked these days so I have taken the opportunity to nominate a saint for each week of the year, thereby rescuing some from total obscurity (and coincidentally providing suggestions for middle-class parents wishing to alienate their children from birth by calling them something stupid).

I hope that you will find this an invaluable resource. However, when I outlined the project to a bishop I know he castigated me as A Bad Person. Sadly, then, this little volume must make its way in the cut-throat world of Christian publishing without an episcopal imprimatur.

While every care has been taken in compiling this work, it remains possible that some small errors may have crept in. If this turns out to be the case, then I hope you will, with a heart of compassion and deep caring, feel free to write me an irritating, nit-picking, hairsplitting little carping letter, and I will gladly ignore it in the same generous spirit.

Yours, from the Vicarage,
Catherine Fox

ORDINARY TIME

SUNDAY OF CHRIST THE KING

or

LAST SUNDAY AFTER PENTECOST

or

LAST SUNDAY AFTER TRINITY

or

Fifth Sunday before Christmas

or

SUNDAY NEXT BEFORE ADVENT

or

Stir-up Sunday

(Green)

This is the day, one week before Advent begins, when the pious of yesteryear—inspired by the beginning of the day's collect, "Stir up, O Lord, the hearts of your faithful people"—used to make their Christmas cakes and puddings. I was brought up a Baptist, so this tradition passed me by. Besides, baking? On the Sabbath? I think not. The wrath of God might strike you in various nasty culinary ways, as detailed in my grandmother's recipe book, which lists more ways in which a cake can fail than King Alfred ever heard of. "Collapsed cake", "collapsed cake with heavy streak at bottom", "collapsed cake with thick greasy crust", "collapsed top with white speckles and sides that fall in", "hole under top crust", or a "close texture".

Grandma was a great cook and had no patience with me for using Jus-Rol frozen puff pastry. "I don't know why you don't make your own, Catherine. All you do is roll the dough out, put the chopped up butter on, fold up the dough, turn it over, roll it into an oblong, fold it in three, give it a half turn to the left, repeat, leave it in a cool place then do it all over again six times. It's terribly easy."

Being Baptists we lived in an alcohol-free household. This meant that we never had a flaming Christmas pudding. (By which I mean a pudding *flambé*, rather than we never flaming well had a Christmas pudding.) And it was years before I learnt about putting booze in cakes. One friend, married to a GP, injects her cake with a syringe full of brandy. Another friend, a midwife, keeps a chart by her cake noting the date and how many mls of alcohol it's had. Being a vicar's wife I estimate how much I'm going to need, administer it, then reverently consume what's left over.

"I think the Vicar needs more coffee not more Cake, mother."

All that then remains is The Ordeal of Covering the Cake. A swift glance at Grandma's book reveals that there are more pitfalls than accidentally eating all the marzipan beforehand.

Great culinary disasters of our time

One Stir-up Sunday disaster struck the vicarage. Owing to a lack of small pudding basins, I ended up attempting to boil a monster pudding in a too-small saucepan without a proper lid. I had to improvise by using a metal pie dish.

Curiously, as the boiling commenced I realized I had accidentally invented the culinary equivalent of liposuction (patent pending). All the suet was slowly syphoned out of the pudding into the water. After an hour or so I heard a loud crash. I immediately stomped to my sons' room and accused them. They looked up from where they were quietly drawing at a desk and denied all knowledge. I went to the kitchen and thought, "That darn pudding's boiled dry." There seemed to be some fat on the floor (good for skating across in woolly socks) but it wasn't till everything had cooled down an hour later that I went back and thought, "What are all those white splashes everywhere?" The answer, dear reader, was suet. Some of it had travelled, don't ask me how, a good three yards from the pan. I tell you, the fall-out was over the entire kitchen. I can only assume that during the blast, the metal pie dish lid was blown up in the air and landed in place again afterwards. I still don't know how I did it. Maybe I failed to recite the collect properly, or perhaps I stirred the mixture widdershins, or maybe (as we don't believe in that superstitious nonsense) it was simply the will of God.

Typo of the week

"THE WOK OF GOD." (AS IN "STIR-FRY, O LORD,
THE HEARTS OF YOUR PEOPLE.")

Saint of the week

ENFLEDA (6TH C), ABBESS OF WHITBY. FEAST: 24 NOVEMBER.

SEASON
OF
ADVENT

FIRST SUNDAY IN ADVENT

or

ADVENT SUNDAY

or

Fourth Sunday before Christmas
(Violet)

Everyone moans about the pre-Christmas rush, but for clergy the phrase "The run-up to Christmas" has a real ring to it. It's a bit like "Exam term" for students. The aim is to pace yourself so that you don't quite collapse until you get back home after the main Christmas service. With shaking hand you accept the glass of sherry lovingly poured by your spouse. You sink with a whimper onto the sofa. At this point, with immaculate timing, the doorbell rings and some poor soul needing accommodation and food will be on your doorstep to test your discipleship to its outer limits. "Just push off!" you think. Then the phrase "No room at the inn" rises up to accuse you.

One Advent a few years back we had The Great Candle Drama in church. A vicar I know bought *purple* advent candles. And with one voice the congregation said, "Oh, vicar, that makes a pleasant change!" Actually, I made that up. They all said, "But vicar, we always have red candles!" At theological college ordinands are trained not to think, "IT'S MY CHURCH AND I'LL DO WHAT I LIKE." Instead you learn to listen respectfully and nod, *then* do what you like.

This year our church will be having an Advent ring with a difference. A vicar I know wanted a great big solid-looking affair with thumping great big Paschal candles. (Ooh, we've never had Paschal candles during Advent before, vicar!) He wanted them purple to go with the new Advent service book covers. He's big on colour co-ordination. My friend the Revolutionary Communist thinks I've basically married a girl. Many male clergy are in touch with their feminine side. (If a surplice is not a big girl's blouse, then I don't know what is.)

After a long and fruitless search he eventually phoned up a vestments firm who also sell candles, mozzettas, picts, morsels, daiquiries, robinias and other things we Evangelicals need know nothing about. These good people dipped the white candles and made them purple at 50p extra a time, so we got the colour co-ordinated look we were after.

This has thrown up a minor musical problem. In the past this vicar I know has got the congregation singing an Advent song to the tune of "The holly and the ivy". The chorus goes "The holly and the ivy / are dancing in a ring / round the berry-bright red candles / and the bright and shining king." The third line no longer works and neither, somehow, does "Round the whopping purple candles". In the end we decided to ditch the ditty altogether. Well, it was a high-church thing, anyway. The vicar had already added a verse to the one about the virgin which stated sternly that "Candle four is ALSO FOR GOD'S PEOPLE".

These are a few of my least favourite things

Christmas round-robins

Every year we are plagued with circular letters detailing the massive achievements of family members and their exciting holidays abroad. They are always written in a strangely impersonal reporting style, never in the first person. And they have LOTS (!!!) of exclamation marks!! But what annoys me most are the ones which take it upon themselves to remind me of the "true meaning" of Christmas. I *know* the true meaning of Christmas. I'M A VICAR'S WIFE!!! All I can manage is a sentence or two of scrawl inside the card to the effect that we are all still alive and that while my older son has passed no violin exams, won no scholarships, nor scored any winning goals in anything whatsoever, he can now burp the entire alphabet. The boy will go far. Propelled by a blast of gastric air, no doubt.

"*I'm sorry Mrs Siddleigh-Barkup,
but these pews are for purple. Alarming Mango is in
the North Transept under our Lady of Veils.*"

Great culinary disasters of our time

A word of warning about mulled wine. After you've mulled it there will be all kinds of debris floating around on the top. You may wish to strain it. Make sure you strain it into a large jug, not down the sink, or you will find yourself staring at a sieve full of cinnamon sticks and orange peel thinking, "I didn't mean to do that, did I?"

Saint of the week

TUDWAL (6TH C), WELSH BISHOP. FEAST: 1 DECEMBER.

SECOND SUNDAY IN ADVENT

or

ADVENT 2
Third Sunday before Christmas
(Ember Days, Wednesday, Friday
and Saturday)

(If devices are provided for the connection
of dust extraction and collection facilities,
ensure these are connected and
properly used.)

(Violet)

═══════════════

Judging by the TV you'd think Christmas was next week. The adverts on children's ITV are reaching fever pitch. It's interesting to notice the strict demarcation between boys' toys and girls' toys. Nowhere is this seen more clearly than in the two rival worlds of Action Man and Barbie.

I still remember the first year I went to buy an Action Man. I was horrified. The things are armed to the teeth! "Don't you have a non-violent Action Man?" I begged the assistant in my hand-wringing liberal kind of a way. "Well, we've got Extreme Sport Action Man," she replied. "He only has a small pistol." For Olympic target shooting, I told myself. All the others had guns and bazookas and what looks like portable bacon slicers; or else they REALLY THROW GRENADES!

Contrast this with the lovely sugar-and-spice world of Her Royal Pinkness, Barbie. Oh, jewel-haired mermaid Barbie! Barbie with baby sister Kelly in a buggy to nurture! Oh, Barbie with boyfriend Miami Ken in spangly trunks whose hair REALLY CHANGES COLOUR! I once bought Ken for my god-daughter. My son, three at the time, examined him closely. "He doesn't look like a real man," he said in disgust. "He doesn't have nipples." Just between you and me, that's not all he doesn't have. Which is perhaps why we never see Single Mum Barbie.

But where will these gender specific toys lead? Are we breeding up a generation of violent men? Or of ultra-feminine women who will rush around in pink frilly housecoats shouting, "Don't throw grenades in here—I've just hoovered!" I was reassured by my son's reaction to his Christmas present. Action Man's favourite occupation was… sitting in his house reading a book. *In*action Man, maybe?

Christmas hint lists

This is the time of year when national newspapers, having decided that we are a useless bunch of timewasters, issue lists of Christmas present suggestions. These are helpfully divided up into types, like "Teenager", "Mother", "Grandparent". I was interested to see that *The Times* thought we mothers might enjoy a silver-plated glass water jug. Well, I might indeed; but possibly not *quite* as much as I'd enjoy having the £220 to spend on clothes.

Children drop hints about what they want from mid-September onwards. I've learnt that the most important words a mother can utter during Advent are, "We'll see." It is profoundly theological, pointing up the eschatological already/not yet tension inherent in our faith. Better still, it annoys the hell out of them. When your child says, "Mum, what I really *really* want for Christmas is a robotic arm that can pick things up and magnetize them," don't rush to Hamley's and buy one. Two days later they really *really* want a lego chrome crusher or Pokemon silver. I must confess that I was a bit disappointed my older son decided against the robotic arm. It sounded like just the thing to break the ice at the Deanery Christmas party. You could put it on the coffee table and watch as it goosed people and magnetized their underwired bras.

Xmas

At this time of year we also start to see the abbreviation of Christmas that irritates practising Christians so much—Xmas. This irritation is misplaced, really, since X is the Greek letter *chi* that is at the beginning of *Christos*. "Xmas" is therefore a deeply Christian abbreviation. We don't need to "put the Christ back into Xmas"—it's already there. The truly Protestant thing to do is to campaign to take the "mass" out of the Festival of Christ's Birth. Just as the truly pagan thing would be to remove all traces of Christianity from the ancient festival of Yuletide.

These are a few of my least favourite things

Toys of a thousand parts

What I'm really hoping this year is that we get no more toys-of-a-thousand parts. I operate a callous hoovering regime. If it's on the floor after my final warning, bad luck. Ah, that satisfying clatter! Then the backlash of guilt and the picking through the dustbag. But anyone who's trodden barefoot on small toys knows how I feel. Perhaps I should follow the advice I once overheard my older son giving the younger (who was yelping because of the lego): "It's all right—just tread on the books."

Saint of the week

WOLFEIUS (?11TH C), FIRST HERMIT OF ST BENET HULME (NORFOLK).
FEAST: 10 DECEMBER.

THIRD SUNDAY
IN ADVENT

or

ADVENT 3

Second Sunday before Christmas

(Note that the Collect appointed for every Sunday, or for any Holy-day that hath a Vigil or Eve, shall be said at the Evening Service next before)

(From 17 December [O Sapientia] begin the eight days of prayer before Christmas Day) (Violet)

⸻

Hurry hurry! This is Advent 3. Only one more Sunday before Christmas! About now a tide of cosmic pointlessness sweeps over me. All those carefully selected gifts—what will become of them? Children, in particular, are fickle in their affections. Take dinosaurs.

Dinosaurs, as every parent knows, belong to a very specific era (after diggers and tractors but before video games) which spans about 18 months of a developing boy's life. During this period these mighty reptiles roam the walls, floors and dinner plates of every home in Britain. They congregate in family groups under pillows and on bath edges, while their near relations, the pterasaurs swoop fearlessly over bannisters onto unsuspecting adults below who emit the characteristic yelp of pain typical of Homo sapiens donked on the head by a lump of hard plastic.

But in less than two years their reign is over. Their remains lie undisturbed in the bottom of plastic toy crates under layers of duplo. The last stragglers are trampled by passing adults—and we hear, yet again, that familiar yelp of pain so evocative of bare-footed Homo sapiens treading on sharp plastic on their way to the loo at 3 am.

What brought about this mass extinction of a once invincible race of beasts? It is one of the most fascinating mysteries of child development. Some extinctions are easier to explain. I will confess (hush, hush, whisper who dares) to the occasional culling of soft toys. But let's face it, some teddies, like turkeys, *are* just for Christmas, not for life. The boys don't notice. They don't name them all the way my sisters and I used to as children. Occasionally some toys are called after the people who gave them; hence a fluffy blue bunny called Keith and a strange trio of knitted cats called Mrs Ethel Watterson.

The Nativity Play

No Christmas would be complete without a children's nativity play. My three sisters and I used to mount Christmas productions each year for my parents, who were always unaccountably reluctant to watch them. We must have persuaded them on one occasion as they report that my youngest sister, playing baby Jesus, lay in the crib whining, "I want my fwankincense, I want my fwankincense!" until eventually, the gentle virgin mother (my big sister) exploded, "Oh all right! *Have your blooming frankincense!*"

There's tremendous scope for nativity plays to plunge into comedy. I've been told about one considerate Joseph tapping his wife on the shoulder and saying, "Wake up, Mary. You've had a baby." You've probably all heard about the innkeeper getting his revenge for being passed over for the part of Joseph: "Of course we've got a room! Come on in." But what about the quick-witted Joseph who glanced round and replied, "I'm not staying in this dump. Come along, Mary. I'd rather sleep in the stable."

Out of the mouths of babes

Carols can be a bit baffling for the average small child. My younger sister was convinced that one of them went "Hairy Demption's happy dawn". I remember being mystified by the Advent hymn "On Jordan's banks the Baptists cry". Why were we all crying, exactly, I used to wonder. Was the Jordan just a tragic place?

What to buy the vicar for Christmas

Some of you may be scratching your heads and wondering what to buy the vicar for Christmas. Crates of claret, vintage cars, villas in Tuscany—all of these are acceptable. Some vestments catalogues are a useful resource. I saw the one once which even sold pyjamas and underpants. Personally, I couldn't actually see anything about the pants that would have precluded a lay person wearing them, but it was a Catholic catalogue, so what do I know? Perhaps there was some sacerdotally significant ratio of cotton to lycra that would pass a Protestant by.

Saint of the week

BEAN, IRISH HERMIT. FEAST: 16 DECEMBER.

FOURTH SUNDAY IN ADVENT

or

ADVENT 4

The Sunday next before Christmas
(Violet)

_This morning I went on a spree in Pound Land where I bought two small artificial Christmas trees for my sons. They can decorate them in any way they wish on the condition that they never again, in the hearing of people with tinsel-decked trees, ask, "Mummy, _why_ do you think tinsel's vulgar?"

My older son has hung up some cardboard stars and motifs cut from wrapping paper while my younger son has decorated his tree a little more unconventionally with lego, bits of spirograph and yellow Action Man boots. He also wanted some toffee wrappers, which would have entailed eating the toffees, of course, but I said, "Certainly not! You've brushed your teeth."

I discovered earlier that they were filling-wrenchingly hard, but I hit upon the brilliant idea of softening them up a bit by crossing my legs and tucking them behind my knee while I read my book. This is sort of biblical. If you remember, Abraham had his servant place a hand under his thigh before swearing an oath in Genesis 24. Interestingly, swearing an oath is exactly what you find yourself doing 45 minutes later when the melted toffee has escaped from its wrapper and welded your jeans legs together.

These are a few of my least favourite things

Carol singers

Do door-to-door carol singers annoy you? They only ever seem to mumble "Wishoo a merry Chrismus and a nappy New Year" while sticking their hand out for cash. My rule is this: I only give money to carol singers collecting for charity. Though having said that, if they turned up and sung a proper carol with harmonies, I might relent. I dare say I wouldn't turn away a cathedral choir empty handed. Instead we get tone-deaf, eight-year-old entrepreneurs.

A vicar I know has a different, and possibly less Scrooge-like, rule. One year he experimented with opening the door swiftly and getting in first with "We wish you a merry Christmas" before demanding money from the open-mouthed youths on the doorstep. This year he waits politely till they've finished then

"We're avoiding the Christmas rush."

asks, "And what *are* the 'glad tidings'?" One little girl told him it was just a song, it didn't mean anything. He said, "If you can tell me what it means, I'll give you 20p." She ran off to consult dad at the end of the drive, came back, rang the doorbell and said, "The brotherhood of man and being kind to everyone?" "No." Off she ran. After a long pause the doorbell rang a third time and she said despairingly: "Jesus was born?" She got her 20p.

Great culinary disasters of our time

This took place several years ago when my sons were both little and I was locked in a kind of permanent Joyce Grenfell sketch. I was being a real mother for once and making Christmas gingerbread dough with my little boys. "Don't eat that… Aargh! Don't spit it back in! Oh, never mind. Just stir it around a bit." We were just at the sifting-flour-in stage ("Look! Snow!" "Not on his head!") when I suddenly remembered the bicarb. I scoured the cupboard—a slightly nasty task, you never know what you'll find—and gave up in despair. "Mummy must have used it all! Silly Mummy! Let's go to the shop." I marched the children up the road, but the shop didn't have any. "Let's try baking powder!" I said brightly. "You said it wouldn't work," I was reminded. Hah!

And then on Sunday night I went to the cupboard and there was the bicarb. I've gone mad, I decided; but before I said, "Oh well" and cracked open the Christmas malt, I did just ask a vicar I know. "You didn't take the bicarb, did you?" A guilty look crossed his face. He'd wrapped it up and used it in a fake Christmas cracker at a children's talk.

What can be learnt from this? I think we can recycle it as a sermon illustration for the kingdom of God. Bicarbonate of soda—it may look like an unimportant thing nobody would miss, but it makes all the difference in the world to gingerbread.

Saint of the week

WINNIBALD (6TH C), ABBOT OF HEIDENHEIM.
BROTHER OF WILLBALD AND WALBURGA. FEAST: 18 DECEMBER.

SEASON
OF
CHRISTMAS

THE NATIVITY OF OUR LORD

or
The Birth-day of Christ

Commonly Called
CHRISTMAS DAY
(The days after Christmas Day until
Epiphany traditionally form a unity
of days of special thanksgiving)

(White or gold)

Here in the vicarage we lie to our children. We tell them that Santa brings the Christmas presents. Actually, Santa's only a kind of glorified delivery boy. The soap comes from Aunty Ethel, the lego from Grandma, but Santa is the one who struggles round the entire world delivering presents to the correct address. Our older son rumbled the truth several years ago, and I'm afraid his little brother is also smelling a rat. "Is Santa magic?" "Yes." "How come, when there's no such thing as magic?"

I'm all for a bit of pretence, so long as Santa isn't used as a threat. I overheard one harrassed woman in a shop snarling to her children, "Right! That's IT it." (As opposed to just "it", I expect.) "There's no way Santa's coming now!" Santa is a free-grace kind of a bloke in our house. He brings gifts regardless of whether we deserve them.

Things would be a lot easier for Santa—and all of us—if next year were declared the Chinese Year of the Voucher. Trying to guess what people want or need is the season's little game of Russian roulette. The line between buying someone what they clearly need and mortally offending them is a fine one. Why, for instance, do we now have more champagne glasses than any other kind? Do people think we have a champagne lifestyle? Actually, it's more of a cheap Cava lifestyle.

A good friend of mine was given an epilator by her husband. Now this is a bold, not to say suicidal, choice unless it appears explicitly on a hints list. Personally, if any man gave me one I'd be inclined to strap him to a chair and epilate his entire body surface without benefit of local anaesthetic. Mention that to my sons, somebody. I was tucking them up the other night and the little one studied my face carefully and ventured, "Mummy, you have ever such a little beard." The older one hooted in derision. "That's not a beard! That's a moustache!"

These are a few of my least favourite things

The wrong kind of snow

On Boxing Day (or The Feast of St Stephen. *Then shall follow the Collect of the Nativity, which shall be said continually unto New Year's Eve*) we went to Northumberland for a few days. During that time my younger son discovered that snow isn't all it's cracked up to be. Admittedly, this was British Rail snow—the wrong kind. It barely stuck together to make a decent snowball and our snowman was more of a snow heap with a carrot planted on top. Afterwards I heard son two complaining, "I wish snow wasn't cold and that it didn't melt!" Ah, but then it wouldn't be snow, my dear. It would be polystyrene.

What Christmas is all about

I have to admit that what with the snow and everything, we've had a really good traditional Christmas. Here's a little challenge for next year: count the number of times you come across the phrase "That's what Christmas is all about". Usually it refers to the festive custom of trying to find out if the human stomach can actually be made to explode by eating and drinking. Going to the pantomime must also

"And it's a **BIG** Hello to everyone from Feltham Scout Group in the audience tonight—and will the clever clogs who locked Dick Whittington in his dressing room kindly let him out so the show can go on!"

qualify. *Oh* yes it must! We went to see *Dick Whittington* in Newcastle. I prudently avoided sitting next to my older son as I knew he'd spend the whole performance going, "What? What's so funny? What are you laughing at? Tell me, tell me!" at every *double entendre* thrown in for the adults in the audience. I cunningly sat away from a vicar I know as well, so I wouldn't have to explain any references to popular youth culture culled from children's TV. "What? What's that about letting the dogs out? Why are you laughing?" The upshot was I spent the whole time explaining to my younger son that yes, that one was Dick Whittington, the one there with the waistcoat; that King Rat was the baddy and that I didn't know why, people just did hiss when he came on stage; and yes, you're right, Sarah the cook was really a man dressed up as a woman.

Saint of the day

ALBURGA (7TH C), FOUNDER OF WILTON NUNNERY.
FEAST: 25 DECEMBER.

FIRST SUNDAY AFTER CHRISTMAS

or

The Sunday after Christmas Day

or

THE CIRCUMCISION OF CHRIST
(The same Collect, Epistle and Gospel
shall serve for every day after
unto the Epiphany)

(When Christmas Day falls on a
Wednesday and the Presentation of Christ
falls on a Sunday the readings appointed
for Year 1 are always used)

(White or gold)

═══════════════

By now most of you will have performed those post-Christmas duties of writing thank-you letters and standing in the returns queue at M&S.

When I married a vicar I know I realized for the first time how different family Christmas traditions could be. My family give gifts that they think will amuse or ravish the receiver. My in-laws give useful gifts. Each year they phone us to elicit a hint list and to give us hints of their own. For example, my mother-in-law might say, "I think Dad would like (drops voice to barely audible whisper) *blank videos*. Did you catch that?"

Coming from a sensible family like that it was small wonder that a vicar I know was baffled by the first gift he ever got from my mother. He sidled up to me later and said out of the corner of his mouth, "Your mum's given me a book called *Staff Sergeant Moss's Dumbell Exercises*." She later gave him a book of 1920s schoolboy stories called *A Toast Fag*, but by then he'd got the hang of the family sense of humour.

True to our family gift-giving tradition, a vicar I know received from his parents a shirt that fits him and goes with a pair of trousers he already possessed, while my parents gave him a framed motto saying, "God Bless Our Home" and *The Sunday School Guide* from 1874.

Many of the presents sent to my sons look at first glance as though they will occupy small people for hours at a time so that their parents can get on with important things like sleeping. This usually turns out not to be the case. "Mummy, *when* will you help me make my football man?" In the end I relented, if only to prevent him from waving the rubber mould at visiting relatives and saying, "Look what I've got," and seeing a small frisson of shock crossing the adult's face before they registered that it was not, after all, a novelty condom.

So there I was, up to my elbows in plaster. "What a fine performance from the hassled mother! That's one figure already complete! And here comes the second—oh, and his head's come off. What a tragedy! The supporters won't like that!" "Well, obviously it's a player with two halves...."

Bad mother award

Still, school started today for the older one at least. Infants go back tomorrow and for once I got it right. Poor child, he still remembers when we took him to his first day of proper school a week early. There was supposed to be a staggered start. Apparently, there had been a letter. New Year's resolution: to read and extract salient points from school letters, then pin them in a safe place for future reference. Why, *why* is this so difficult? I must—will—study them as I sit with my cup of tea and slice of Christmas cake, absent-mindedly eating fragments of plaster off the table from the football mould which I have mistaken for icing.

Saint of the week

EGWIN (6TH C), BISHOP OF WORCESTER. FEAST: 30 DECEMBER.

NEW YEAR'S DAY

or

1st January

Holy Name of Jesus
or
The Naming of Jesus
or
The Circumcision of Christ

(Mary, Mother of God)

(White)

The 1st of January (when observed as New Year's Day, see *The Revised Common Lectionary*) is a bit of a non-event in the C of E. We operate on two time-scales simultaneously: the church year and the calendar year. Advent is the liturgical New Year. There is no official church celebration of 1st Jan. No watchnight service of the kind other denominations go in for.

I've never cared for New Year's celebrations, really. It's always struck me as peculiar to hang around till midnight and sing "Should auld acquaintance be forgot" with a bunch of drunken half-strangers you'll never meet again, when you'd much rather be in bed. If you watch closely you'll notice that nobody really knows the words. Perhaps the slurring is really an attempt at improvisation, not drunkenness:

> "Should auld acquaintance be forgot
> Le la zzhhve zzvhe mmm-mind?
> Should auld acquaintance be forgot?
> La la la auld lang shyne!?"

I also suspect that people have no idea what the words mean. They think it's saying we *should* forget people, and this puzzles them, though occasionally the suggestion is welcome. And what does your average sassenach make of the line "And we'll tak' a richt gude willy-waught / For auld lang syne"? I consulted the glossary of my National Song Book and it says that a "willy-waught" is a "long draught". The dialect shields us from the sordid truth—this song is nothing more than a rhyming version of the sentiments you get in any pub when men have been drinking freely. "I love you, mate, you're a good pal, another pint for my mate! We go back a long way, you're a brother to me, give ush yer 'and—" *clunk* (sound of head slumping on bar).

Is this any kind of song for a vicar's wife to be singing?

Resolutions

Out with the old, in with the new. Dust off those Lenten vows of self-denial, it's New Year's resolution time. Hands up those of you who have decided to eat more sensibly? One of the saddest ironies of human existence is the fact that we are forever destined to renounce sweets when the house is at its confectionary peak.

Well, there's good news: chocolate is good for you. Yes, it said so in *The Independent*. A study in America found that men who regularly eat sweets and chocolate lived almost a year longer than those who were "good". Naturally, if you say this to your nearest and dearest they will laugh cynically, so a little mugging up is called for. Just practise the following until you can say it in an off-hand kind of way: "As you're probably aware, chocolate contains phenols, which mop up free radicals associated with a wide range of illnesses. Besides preventing the oxidation of low-density lipoproteins, of course."

These are a few of my least favourite things

Dentists

As adults we have to learn to hold in tension a love of sweets with the fear of root-canal fillings. I once told a (sort-of) lie to a dentist. I'd been eating a bag of filling extractors, otherwise known as toffee bonbons, and found myself crunching on something that was definitely not icing sugar. The dentist peered at the damage and asked sternly, "What have *you* been eating?" Fortunately most dentists have the habit of answering their own questions, owing to the fact that they usually spring something on you when they've got half a ton of ironmongery in your mouth. This dentist went on to snort, "Granary bread, I suppose!" I nodded dumbly. Well, I had.

I find that rather a sad cameo, though—all those people diligently chomping their way through granary bread because it's healthy and still ending up in the dentist's chair. You may as well buy a 2lb-box of Thornton's special toffee and *enjoy* laying waste to years of expensive dentistry.

Saint of the day

ODILO (9TH C), ABBOT OF CLUNY. FEAST: 1 JANUARY.

SECOND SUNDAY AFTER CHRISTMAS

or

CHRISTMAS 2

or

DIET SUNDAY
(White or gold)
(Sunday between
2 January and 5 January)

January is always a glum month. The excitement of Christmas is fading behind us. We are all cranky and short-tempered because we are on diets, but we aren't far enough into the New Year to abandon the attempt. What we need is good news. Here we are—tea, according to the latest research, has "greater anti-oxidant properties than most fruits". Take that, you raw spinach freaks! Doctors tell us to eat five portions of fresh fruit and veg a day. That puts many of us in credit at the anti-oxidant bank.

This just goes to show that if you wait long enough all your favourite things will be declared good for you. Still awaiting their healthy-eating clearance are: clotted-cream fudge, crisp butties and, of course, that well-known panacea, a stiff gin with a chunk of lime.

More tea, Vicar?

Every vicarage has its own set of mugs to serve drinks at meetings. Some will be new—jolly mediterranean colours, perhaps. These will be supplemented by the Second Eleven of vicarage mugs, those commemorating parish missions or diocesan Mothers' Union centenaries. After this will come the 39p-each mugs from the Cheapo Shop which repeatedly pose the question, Shall I bother to wash this up, or shall I carelessly drop it on the floor?

The world is divided into those who can take orders for tea and coffee and those who can't. I can't, so a vicar I know has to do it. He can hold in his mind both main types, plus all the caffeinated/decaffeinated, Earl Grey/truckie tea sub categories. Then there's people who drink fruit tea. (Possible gap in the market here for liturgical herbal bags? Pentecost Sizzler? Lenten Bracer?) And there's always one person who mysteriously asks for hot water.

After the meeting the mugs may be stacked in the dishwasher or washed manually and dried with a strange collection of tea towels, some with Year Two St James C of E School on and some accidentally pinched from self-catering retreat houses.

More gin, Vicar?

I occasionally meet people who are under the impression that vicars aren't allowed to drink alcohol.... (That row of dots was to allow time for people who actually know any vicars to roll about in hysterical laughter.) Little misunderstandings like this will arise from time to time. At our last garden party I went round with a large jug offering people rum punch. Some of them said, "Ho, ho, very funny! Go on then." They were later seen wandering in the herbaceous borders and muttering, "I don't know what was in that orange juice...."

If God had intended us to smoke, He would have given us little chimneys on our heads

How far should Christian hospitality extend? I discovered recently that mine founders on the rocky issue of guests smoking in our house. But by issuing a "no smoking" decree, am I also tacitly issuing a "no non-church-types" decree at the same time? My compromise has been to allow our guests to smoke in the dining room, provided they puff out of the French windows, after which I fly round dementedly with my spray can of Fag-off, or whatever it's called. But perhaps the best solution of all would be to say, "You are, of course, welcome to smoke;

but you will have to listen to a lecture on the subject from my older son." At the age of five he had a habit of demanding in pained disbelief, "Mum, *why* do people smoke when they *know* it's bad for them? Is it because they're foolish?" He remains to this day a one-boy government health warning.

Saint of the week

MUNCHIN (7TH C), IRISH BISHOP.
FEAST: 2 JANUARY.

SEASON
OF
EPIPHANY

EPIPHANY OF THE LORD

(6 January or First Sunday in January)
or
The Manifestation of Christ to the Gentiles
(White or gold)

We took our Christmas decorations down on the twelfth day of Christmas, like you're supposed to. Our older son went through the card pile counting up the number of "wrongs"—pictures showing the shepherds following the star. It was the *wise men* who followed the star, as any fule kno. A great deal of tradition has grown up around the magi, but in truth we can learn very little about them from the Scriptures. English translations tell us that "there came wise *men* from the East", but I see no reason to rule out the possibility that some of them were women. We don't even know how many there were. As few as two, as many as two hundred—no wonder Herod was twitchy. They offered Jesus gifts of gold, frankincense and myrrh. Was that three separate gifts? Or nine gifts, three of each? Or was it one Ikea-style boxed set of three, called *Knut*? Although they brought swanky presents, we can't assume they were kings. Their names only appeared in later folklore. One year my older son told me confidently he knew what they were: "Caspar, Melchior and Dennis."

These are a few of my least favourite things

Disposing of the Christmas tree

I always heave a sigh of relief when Epiphany comes and we can finally take down the Christmas decorations and haul the Christmas tree out onto the drive. Eventually we'll take it to the dump. When we lived in Gateshead people used to leave them out on the street so that they could blow under car wheels. I notice that the local custom here is less fun-loving. Most people seem to shove the trees nose-down in their wheelie-bin. I'm half-intending to keep ours till next year and spray it green.

Many people sensibly opt for artificial trees, but I need the smell of Norway spruce before I feel truly Christmassy. My mother has an artificial tree with authentic needle-shedding effect, which must be the worst of both worlds. But the final scraps have now been hoovered up for the year.

Favourite cracker toy of the year

While hoovering I rescued a slip of paper which read: "Puzzle ball. Let's take apart and enjoy assembling. 1. Hold A1 hand put A2 and A3 on both side of A1. 2. Slide B1 and B2 on both side of A2 and A3. 3. Slide C1 for the side of B1 through the side of B2." This kept us entertained for quite a while on Christmas Day, since none of the pieces were numbered and all were identical. A parable of life, I fear.

FIRST SUNDAY AFTER EPIPHANY

or

Baptism of Our Lord

or

The Baptism of Christ

EPIPHANY 1
(Green from Monday)
(Or white)
(unless you are Schedule D self-employed)

═══════════════════

I heard today about a man whose excellent dentist moved to Greece, so twice a year he gets on a plane and flies to Greece for his check-up. Is this someone with money to burn? I have trouble just paying the dentist on top of a 55p bus fare. Sometimes I dither in the waiting room, wondering if it would be cheaper in the long run to pop home and get pregnant in order to qualify for free dental care. How many root-canal fillings add up to the cost of rearing a child?

Maybe the man was just finding a way to manage his fear of dentists. You find one you trust and you stick to him/her come hell, high water and six-monthly trips to Athens. It's worth it to feel you're in safe hands. Dentistphobia is a common complaint. Some people are only mildly afflicted, others are rigid with terror at the very thought. Strictly speaking, it isn't a genuine phobia, since phobias are irrational fears. Being afraid of pain is totally rational in my book. It only becomes a phobia when you are more scared of your friendly local dentist than of the pain of toothache. I read once about a man who preferred to pull his own teeth out with pliers than take a ride in Mr Smith's uppy-downy chair. Now *that's* a phobia. My way of coping is to tell myself it can't be as bad as labour. (Although I did comfort myself in the delivery suite with the thought that it couldn't be as bad as a root-canal filling.)

For many people the real fear is to do with injections. (Will the needle in the roof of my mouth emerge out of the top of my head?) And for these people, there is good news! I saw it in the paper. A new needle-free method of administering injections is being developed. Something to do with shooting bolts of high pressure frozen gas into your skin. Is it just me, or does that sound even more scary than needles?

"Nurse will just give you something to knock you out now..."

These are a few of my least favourite things

Spiders

One of the things I dread is the cry of, "Mu-u-um, there's a spider in our room." I appreciate that spiders do a good and useful job, and provided they keep themselves to themselves, we can co-exist reasonably well. Small spiders I can deal with humanely, but I have a cut-off point at around 1.5cm in diameter (including legs). Once, recently, I inspected a spider and found that it fell just outside the acceptable range, so permission was given to interrupt Daddy in the PCC officers' meeting. A form of words was agreed upon: "Mummy says, please will you come and deal with the spider in our bedroom?" But alas! The message came back, "Put a glass over it and I'll deal with it later."

I can usually manage this initial stage of spider disposal, unless they're huge, in which case I'm worried I might leave a leg sticking out, or worse, that the spider will hurtle angrily round the room with the glass riding on its back like a demented tortoise. But with the best will in the world, I cannot put a glass over a spider which is on the ceiling. In the end the vicar had to come up anyway (and picked it up in his hand, shriek!) as I was nerving myself with tumbler and interflora leaflet.

Saint of the week

KENTIGERNA (8TH C), ANCHORESS. FEAST: 7 JANUARY.

"*That's a very kind offer, madam. But, unfortunately, queen's regulations don't permit Anchoresses, commissioned or otherwise.*"

SECOND SUNDAY AFTER EPIPHANY

or

EPIPHANY 2

(Green)

(or white)

―――――――――

efore long we will be returning to Ordinary Time, or what passes for it, here in the vicarage. There is no mistaking the oddness of our existence as a clergy family. Even if you removed the sign saying "The Vicarage", there would still be dozens of things lying about the house that would give the game away. Here is a random selection.

1. *Christian paperbacks.* Why? Why so many? Does anyone ever read them more than once? If not, why can nobody bring themselves to bin them? Hands up if you still have wholesome Christian marriage manuals from the seventies on your shelves, called something like *Blessed Submission: The Joy of Male Headship*, or *Jesus Wants Me for a Doormat*? And what about all those incredible life testimony books? Can you read them without wondering why God never works miracles like that in your life/church? And books with titles like *Know What You Believe And Why*. There's nothing like a bookcase full of Christian paperbacks for inducing feelings of rebellion and worthlessness.

2. *Bottles of communion wine with an inch left in the bottom.* Sometimes the vicar's wife nearly, nearly uses it in the trifle if she's run out of sherry, but some obscure liturgical reason always restrains her.

3. *Overhead projector acetates.* Research has shown that no church can grow unless it has an overhead projector.

4. *Old ice-cream tub containing 27 marker pens in assorted colours, none of which really work.*

5. *A4 paper* with page two of photocopied order of service on one side, phone messages (eg "Co-op Fun crem Tues 10.30")/drawings of Batman on the other.

6. *Vast cardboard tomato* used as visual aid for harvest children's talk, which may come in for a school assembly some day.

7. *Fifty mugs* with church logo on left over from centenary celebrations, but useful for meetings.

8. *Two or more clapped-out hi-fis* donated "for the youth club" which haven't yet been taken to the charity shop.

9. *Larry Norman LPs.*

10. *Dog collars.*

Yes, my life is odd. I think it's far harder for vicarage children. After all, I am a consenting adult in oddness. Vicarage children can respond by kicking over the traces, or by embracing the family weirdness whole-heartedly. I think this was what I did as a child. My father was a lay preacher and later a Baptist minister. I may be different, I used to think, but that's because I'm *better*. Looking back I can see that this was *not ideal*, but it helped me cope. I was lamenting to a vicar I know about how impossible it is to protect our children from the harshness of the world. He said, "Yes, but we can point them to the one sure refuge." And I, in my odd way, burst into tears.

These are a few of my least favourite things

Drains

We have a problem with drains here at the vicarage. I should have realized, I suppose, when I overheard someone remarking that the previous vicar was "forever rodding the drains". I was struck by the expression. It made drain-rodding sound like a hobby. My informant told me that our predecessor even had his own set of rods. Now I know why. He wasn't just doing it for fun. Five minutes to fill, I know, I'll rod the drains. *There is a problem with these drains.* This came to light recently when half our electricity mysteriously went off.

The electrician sent by the diocese pulled up a couple of floorboards and located the problem—a cable and junction box submerged under inches of water. The water was pumped out, but when the diocesan builder peered into the drains he summoned Dynorod. Now there's a macho-sounding name. I found myself wondering what a group of all-women rodders might call themselves. Femi-rod? He then said my husband would be well advised to buy his own set of rods. Something for the Christmas hints list.

Saint of the week

FURSEY (7TH C), IRISH ABBOT. FEAST: 16 JANUARY.

THIRD SUNDAY AFTER EPIPHANY

or

EPIPHANY 3
Fed-up Sunday
(Green)
(or white)

One of the gloomiest things about your average vicarage is the carpets. This is because carpets are expensive. Any time clergy move jobs they are given a diocesan resettlement allowance. We refer to this as the diocesan carpet allowance, or rather, rug allowance.

So we put up with the carpets we find already waiting for us, the ones our predecessors mysteriously didn't take with them. These will combine two characteristics: first, they will be too good simply to throw out; secondly, they will be almost, but not quite, too vile to live with. I'm talking about patterned carpets. You know—the exploding cabbage kind. You would almost, almost rather walk on bare boards, except when you've got small children.

But let's not forget the clergy talent for spotting the non-existent silver lining. It goes something like this: We have plum-coloured armchairs. We move house. The entire downstairs is carpeted in loathsome mustard-yellow and ochre-splodge carpet (ex office, very good quality). Thinks: Hmm. Plum and mustard. We can work with this.... At least it's not orange. Maybe we could make some yellow-and-wine coloured patchwork cushions to unite the themes?

What you must never do is articulate to yourself the thought, "I hate this carpet!" What you *must* do is insure it, just in case you ever have a burst pipe. This happened to us, and because the vile mustard was top quality Wilton we now have amazing *plain* carpets in colours we actually chose. The next people who move in will go: Hmm. Plum carpet. We have a brown suite. Never mind. We can work with this....

These are a few of my least favourite things

Vicarage curtains

There is a rule about vicarage curtains which comes into play when you move house. If you live in a vicarage with wide shallow windows, your next house will have tall thin windows, and vice versa. There will probably be some curtains in the windows kindly left by your predecessor. Unfortunately, they will be the sort that double as robes for the wise men in the nativity play, rather than the kind of thing that you'd actually pick out voluntarily. "Catherine Fox is lucky to have curtains at all"—if you're thinking this, please call round and collect a set of mustard nylon cast-offs and see how lucky you feel a week later.

The main thing about vicarage windows is that you want to discourage people from peering in to see if you're having tantric sex. We never do, by the way. The vestments get all tangled. (Oh, and it's Buddhist.) This degree of privacy can be achieved either by nets or by the cheaper expedient of never washing your windows. In any case, bright shiny windows are cruel. Birds zonk into them and kill themselves.

Public and private

Vicarages are not like other homes. They have a public aspect—this is where the vicar's study is, where the PCC standing committee meets and where gonks are ingeniously constructed for fancywork stalls. But at the same time they are private family homes where the vicar and spouse eat, have rows, shout at their offspring and fail to have tantric sex (at any rate until the Anglican Church sets up a dialogue with Tantrism).

The vicarage downstairs loo (there's always an upstairs one, too) is where public and private realms collide. You can't treat it as your own private family space and fill it with dodgy cartoon books and

"Ah, Bishop, you've um...oh dear...
your crozier?"

'humorous' postcards. You have to bear in mind that at any time your smallest room might be requisitioned for church use. My rule of thumb is—What if the bishop called? Would my loo disgrace me? Would he have to kick aside ancient potties, wade through miles of unravelled loo paper, and finally encounter a scuba-diving action man bobbing in the pan? What kind of decor is welcoming for the episcopal visitor? Lots of heavy brocades, gilt candlesticks, incense, musical loo seat which plays "O Jesus I have promised", mirror to check the mitre and a handy place to prop a crozier.

Saint of the week

TORTGITH (7TH C), NUN OF BARKING. FEAST: 26 JANUARY.

ORDINARY TIME

FOURTH SUNDAY AFTER EPIPHANY

or

EPIPHANY 4

or

(The Fourth Sunday before Lent)

(If the result is a loss, enter this in box 3.80 and '0' in box 3.79 unless you have claimed farmer's averaging)

(Green)

Although we aren't actually ordained ourselves, the role of clergy wife is a sacred calling. Special qualities are required. Sadly, these are not conferred by the laying on of episcopal hands. We have to scramble them together as best we can. They include:

1. Omniscience

You have to know everything without actually being told it. Eg. the phone rings. You answer, and a voice says, "Oh, could you just tell the vicar it's all right, we found the nurse's umbrella, it was in the vestry all along." You know nothing of the nurse or the umbrella. You don't even know who's calling, but you promise to pass the message on in a voice which implies you are completely *au fait* with the situation.

2. Mendacity

You shouldn't actually lie unless it's unavoidable, but you will frequently have to mislead, evade or smile politely under adverse circumstances. Eg. You are screaming at the children as you try to thrust them in the car, you crack your head on the car door and drop the keys in the gutter. *Parishioner* (passing by): "How are you?" *You* (clutching head, smiling politely): "Fine, fine. And you?" (Whoever you are) *Parishioner:* "Not so good. What with last week." *You* (tentatively yet sympathetically): "Mmm. Mmm. It must have been hard for you...."

3. GSOH (as they say in the personal columns)

Without a sense of humour you're sunk.

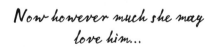

If being a vicar's wife is bad, imagine being a bishop's wife. Think of all those confirmations. You arrive and sit on your own near the front. At first people ignore you, because they don't know you're someone important, if only by proxy. Then somebody asks, and you admit you're the bishop's wife. They will recoil with the words, "Oh! I'm so sorry!" Then comes the problem of what to do when your husband processes down the aisle. In some Evangelical churches he will be applauded. In high churches they might well genuflect. Now, however much she may love him, a bishop's wife will think, "I'm not clapping. And I'm *certainly* not genuflecting!"

Now however much she may love him...

These are a few of my least favourite things

Tutters

There are two types of tutters. First, charismatic tutters, who tut affirmingly during extempore prayer: "Oh Lord (tut), we just want to thank you (tut)...." Then there are worldly tutters who tut nastily when small children howl, run about or bash their parents' keys loudly on the wooden floor. I was once sitting in church with my (then) noisy baby behind a premier league tutter. She turned round to tut at us, then saw that the noisemaker was the vicar's son. Her snarl turned to an "ah, bless him!" smile. There seems to be some fondly held myth among women of a certain age that children in the good old days used to know how to behave in church. Certainly *their* children never made a sound.

I can imagine nothing more off-putting to a visitor who has struggled to church with her children, than an army of disapproving tutters. If the church is the body of Christ, then these people are the appendix—no known purpose other than to grumble and make things uncomfortable for everyone else.

Typos of the week

"THINKING OF RUNNING AN ALPHA CURSE?"
"DAVID USED TO ACCOMPANY HIS PSALMS ON A PARP."
"FAKE MY LIFE AND LET IT BE."
NOT FORGETTING THE OLD FAVOURITE
"GIVE ME OIL IN MY LAP, KEEP ME BURNING."

Saint of the week

JULIAN THE HOSPITALLER (MYTHICAL),
PATRON SAINT OF INNKEEPERS, BOATMEN AND TRAVELLERS.
FEAST: 29 JANUARY.

FIFTH SUNDAY AFTER EPIPHANY

or

NINTH SUNDAY BEFORE EASTER
(Third Sunday before Lent)

or

THE SUNDAY CALLED SEPTUAGESIMA

(Green)

These days it is possible to live quite reasonably on a clergy stipend, unless you've got loads of children. In the old days clergy wives had to count every last copper and forage for bilberries out on the moors.

People like to give vittals to vicars. If you live in the country you might get given a brace of pheasants at Christmas—unplucked, ungutted, so not for the squeamish. Usually, however, you get rhubarb and marrows. At Christmas you might also get booze. If you don't, why not pal up with a GP and scrounge some of his/her surplus malt whisky? Or else invite lots of people round for dinner. In Evangelical circles people generally bring more wine than they consume, so you should have a bottle or two left over.

An atmosphere of waste-not-want-not still lingers on in those of us who grew up as PKs (preachers' kids). We remember things like not using the top of the milk, because it was supposed to go in a little jug as "cream". We knew not to go and make ourselves a bacon sandwich as those last two rashers were probably the basis of a nutritious meal for seven people. We saw the logic behind the butter-or-jam rule. We ate stuffed marrow. We ate baked marrow. We ate marrow risotto. We ate marrow and ginger jam. This is why we feel obscurely furtive and defiant when we buy dry cured bacon. What's wrong with streaky vacuum packed, eh? Or bacon pieces? It's also why we can't simply throw out the chicken carcass. We put it in the fridge in an empty ice-cream tub, intending to use it for soup. Of course, we throw it out two weeks later when it's gone mouldy, but we still can't quite bring ourselves to bypass the fridge and dump it straight in the bin.

Great church traditions

The bunfight

In recent years I've had the privilege of experiencing high-church worship at close quarters. It's given me the chance to discern those things which are central to our faith and those which are simply a matter of taste. One of the central things is the church bunfight. These differ according to churchmanship and region, but all churches have them. Here is an account of the main differences between a bunfight in North Oxford (high) and Gateshead (low).

In Oxford people used to bring in things like Italian bread with olives and sundried tomatoes, cous-cous salad reeking of garlic and fresh basil, hummous, kettle chips, raw vegetable cruditées and dips, carrot cake and so on. There was usually wine.

In Gateshead the pastry cook reigned supreme. Wall-to-wall quiche with sausage rolls, pasties, custard tarts, apple pies and mince pies. I was caught out by the latter early on. Ooh, I could just fancy a mince pie, I thought, it being a long time since Christmas. It turned out to be minced *beef*. No fancy foreign bread here. This is the land of the stottie. And no nonsense about sugar and cholesterol either. For me it was a wonderful return to the Sunday school parties of my childhood when I would eat sixteen sausage rolls and twenty-three chocolate finger biscuits and then be sick during musical bumps.

The only disappointment is that you don't get wine, you get a *nice cup of tea*. But the biggest difference of all between north and south is that in Oxford the table was picked bare. Twenty minutes after the off it looked as though a plague of locusts had swept through leaving only one sprig of bent cress behind. In Gateshead overcatering

"Oi, Doreen, ain't there supposed to be twelve baskets full of left-overs? I'm five short!"

was the name of the game. It wasn't a proper bunfight if a good 30–50% wasn't left over. Everyone took a bag full home—or an empty ice-cream tub full. You could always use the box for dud marker pens later on.

Saint of the week

TRUMWINE (8TH C), BISHOP OF ABERCORN. FEAST: 10 FEBRUARY.

SIXTH SUNDAY AFTER EPIPHANY

or

EPIPHANY 6
(Proper 1, except when this Sunday is
the Last Sunday after the Epiphany)

or

EIGHTH SUNDAY BEFORE EASTER
(Second Sunday before Lent)

or

THE SUNDAY CALLED SEXAGESIMA
(Green)

Another Valentine's Day is almost upon us. Fifty million roses will be sold. Acres of trees will die to make cards. The Thornton's queues will go right round the block. All those odd people who call their partners "Squidgy Bum" or "Piglet" will be placing messages in the national papers. Why?

For once I stopped to wonder who St Valentine was and why he has prompted all this fuss. I checked in my dictionary of saints and discovered that nobody knows. For all I can tell the whole thing could be a conspiracy of stationers, confectioners and florists. Not forgetting the champagne makers and manufacturers of heart-shaped satin cushions, teddies saying, "I wuv 'oo," pink balloons and amusing underpants.

There are two third-century Valentines, one a priest and one a bishop, about whom so little is known that they might even be one and the same person. My book says he/they have no connection with courting couples, but mentions that there is an old tradition that birds pair on 14 February. Alternatively, the custom of choosing a Valentine may be a remnant of the Roman Lupercalia festival (an ancient pagan fertility rite) which took place in mid-February. And there you were, innocently buying a card without realizing you were *blasphemously paying homage to the Roman god of crops.*

I feel it my duty as a clergy wife and upholder of Christian tradition to start an anti-Valentine's Day movement. But just in case I'm called a kill-joy, I shall offer a Christian alternative. February 14 is also the day of Conran, Cyril and Methodius, and Zeno of Rome. I think that gives us plenty of scope. Zeno is patron saint of fishermen, so a nice bit of smoked salmon would make an acceptable Zeno Day gift. Cyril and Methodius are patrons of ecumenists, so how about a fun-packed act of ecumenical worship? Poor old Conran doesn't seem to be patron of anything, so I suggest a shopping spree followed by a slap-up meal in an appropriately named restaurant.

Alternatively, we might concoct scriptural valentines. Be careful, though. I wasn't thrilled one year to read: "I have compared you, my love, to one of Pharaoh's chariot horses."

These are a few of my least favourite things

Vamping the vicar

For many reasons clergy are open to temptation. All too often they are in the position of hearing the intimate problems of their flock, or of having to console them in their grief. Now and then "one thing leads to another" and before we know it we have yet another vicar skeddadling with the organist's wife, or whoever. I have, on occasion, had to protect a vicar I know from excitable female members of the youth group. (I recommend beating them off with a rolled-up newspaper.) I haven't yet worked out what to do about the times when he inspires members of the congregation to pen religious verse. This isn't mentioned in Paul's epistles as one of the gifts of the Spirit, but he seems to possess it, nonetheless. Perhaps I should collect all the offerings and publish an anthology on his retirement to raise money for the Church Urban Fund?

Typos of the week

THIS OCCURRED IN A REPORT ON A CHURCH YOUTH GROUP'S ACTIVITIES: "VARIOUS POUTINGS ABOUT ONCE A MONTH."

Saint of the week

GOBNET (5TH C), VIRGIN. SHE IS SAID TO HAVE PREVENTED A ROBBER FROM BUILDING A CASTLE BY THROWING A STONE BALL ACROSS THE GLEN. PATRON SAINT OF HIGHLAND GAMES AND SMALL BOYS WITH CATAPULTS (?) FEAST: 11 FEBRUARY.

"Turn your radio down, laddie!
Do ye want Gobnet onto us?"

LAST SUNDAY AFTER EPIPHANY

(or Transfiguration Sunday)
(Transfiguration may also be observed
on 6 August)
or
THE SUNDAY CALLED QUINQUAGESIMA
or
SEVENTH SUNDAY BEFORE EASTER
(The Sunday next before Lent)
(Green)

The Transfiguration is not something widely celebrated outside church circles. This is the day when we remember Jesus going up the mountain with a few of his disciples who saw him transformed into a glorious appearance. I believe more could be made of it, as the idea of transformation resonates with ordinary people. How else can we account for the current obsession with home improvement?

When I get restless I dream of what I would do to the house if I unexpectedly went onto the best-seller list. What raw silk curtains we would have then! What acres of (plain) Axminster! What quirky antique Venetian mirrors! In the absence of money the obvious solution is to move the furniture round. About a year after we moved to Walsall a vicar I know helped me carry a sofa upstairs. Our small son saw us and cried out in joy: "Oh! Are we moving back to Gateshead?" The vicar and I looked at one another, sofa balanced dodgily on the banister and thought, Ah. He still thinks this is a temporary aberration which will end as inexplicably as it began and we will return to normal life on Tyneside. Sorry, my son. This is it. This *is* normal life, this that you see going on around you. From now on I'll have to move things round in the dead of night so as not to raise his hopes.

Changing churches

Why this urge to improve the happy home? It's a big money industry at the moment. When I watched *Changing Rooms* for the first time it occurred to me that there might be some mileage in doing a C of E version—"Changing Churches". Picture some hearty Evos from St Jim's standing in St Mary the Virgin. "First of all we want to get rid of all this horrible gloomy dark wood and the tacky statues. We're looking for something bright and airy and flexible. Those pews have got to go. That's quite a nice table, so let's bring it right down into the middle here. The candles are no good—we need some proper lighting."

At the same time down at St Jim's the Spikes are shuddering. "Plastic stacking chairs! No! The whole place looks like a lecture theatre. We're aiming for a much more dramatic look: lots of carved wood, brass candelabra, gorgeous fabrics, subtle lighting. We could easily turn that crèche into a nice intimate little Lady chapel. The wood from the platform could be used to make a reredos quite cheaply. And that overhead projector screen's got to go!"

If the good Lord had meant us to have chairs he wouldn't have created pews

Pew conflict is something that plagues the C of E. It's like some lengthy civil war, with battles and skirmishes being fought in every parish in the land. The rallying cry goes up: "We've always had pews in this church, Vicar" on the one hand. On the other: "What have we got? PEWS! Where do we want them? OUT!" Of course historically the pew is a relative newcomer. But somehow they have become a permanent fixture. Even when they have been ripped out and replaced with chairs, everyone likes to sit in their "own" place, as if occupying some ghostly place memory of a long-gone pew.

"Daddy, it's Becca's turn to sit next to the previous incumbent this morning."

Many turfed-out pews end up in vicarages. This isn't because we nick them, heaven forbid! Rather that we are uniquely well placed to snap them up when they come on the market. The old Victorian varnish on them is nasty but interesting. It's not waterproof and when wet, it sticketh closer than any brother. On rainy days a mighty ripping sound echoes round the building as a damp congregation stands for the first hymn.

Saint of the week

GERTRUDE OF NIVELLES (7TH C), ABBESS.
INVOKED AGAINST PESTS OF RATS AND MICE.
FEAST: 17 MARCH.

SEASON OF LENT

THE FIRST DAY OF LENT COMMONLY CALLED ASH WEDNESDAY

or

The Day after Shrove Tuesday,
commonly called Pancake Day
(Violet [or Lent array])

═══════════

When I was a child we Baptists didn't go in for Lent very much. Other children would talk at school of "giving something up for Lent", but I never quite grasped why. Perhaps if the *ASB* had been written back then I would have learned more about DAYS OF DISCIPLINE AND SELF-DENIAL. These include "Ash Wednesday, Good Friday. The other weekdays in Lent." Did you notice that Sundays aren't included? This means there is a legal loophole for chocolate-eaters and wine-lovers. But it has to be off-set against "all the Fridays in the year" (apart from festivals). Liturgical swings and roundabouts, I'm afraid.

There is a broad spectrum of Lenten observation. In Anglo-Catholic circles there are all kinds of arcane rituals about removing things from the church and covering other things up. Evangelicals tend instead to "take something up" for Lent—reading worthy paperbacks, usually.

In the middle ground there is a range of self-denying acts, the giving up of alcohol and chocolate being the most common. But there is a flaw in the reasoning here. Q. Why do we give up chocolate? A. To deny ourselves. But is it that simple? This denial may mask a more sinister motive—that of losing weight and improving the complexion;

in a word, *vanity*. In this godless, superficial age it would surely be a bolder act of self-denial to eat Mars bars until you go up two dress sizes and burst out in unsightly pustules. That would mortify the flesh all right.

"*I'm giving up vanity for Lent.*"

These things are sent to try us

Part of the point of Lenten discipline is to train ourselves up to resist temptation. Back in the good old days they used to say you could tell a vicar's churchmanship by the sin he was accused of. If he was accused of homosexuality, he was high church, if it was adultery, he was broad church. If he was accused of embezzling the funds he was an Evangelical. When you consider the average turnover in the church's financial year the Evangelical option is a bit sad, isn't it?

Let's look at the numerous and subtle temptations which the average vicar must resist:

1. The temptation to punch the next moron who quips, "Got a good job, haven't you? You only work one day a week!"

2. The temptation to say, "I'm sorry, my dad's/the vicar's out," when someone appears on the doorstep wanting the train fare to Glasgow where their granny is dying.

3. The temptation to raid the missionary box when you've run out of cash. Of course, you'll pay it back later....

4. When a parishioner asserts, "I live my life by the ten commandments, me," there's the temptation to enquire, "And those are...?"

5. The urge to buy a tiny discreet radio and listen to England thrashing the Aussies during evensong.

6. The urge to stop devout Catholics in the street on Ash Wednesday and say, "Excuse me, you seem to have a smudge on your forehead."

There are a separate set of temptations reserved for the clergy wife. They can be summed up under the heading "The urge to misbehave". This can find expression in innocuous things like wearing Doc Martens and writing rude words with other people's fridge magnets.

The problem is that people have an antiquated stereotype of vicar's wives. For goodness sake! These days some of us are *men* if the vicar's a woman. Clergy husbands—do you get asked to run stalls at the bazaar? I doubt it. I bet everyone who doesn't know thinks you're the vicar. Women clergy—how often do you open the door and find yourself greeted with the words, "Hello, love. Is the vicar in?"

Saint of the day

THIS WILL DEPEND, OF COURSE, ON WHEN ASH WEDNESDAY FALLS,
WHICH DEPENDS, IN ITS TURN, ON WHEN EASTER IS.
(SEE BELOW, "HOW TO CALCULATE THE DATE OF EASTER".)

FIRST SUNDAY IN LENT

or
LENT 1
(Sixth Sunday before Easter)
(Ember Days: Wednesday, Friday and
Saturday of this week)
(Violet [or Lent array])

═══════════════

How to calculate the date of Easter

You will need:

1. Book of Common Prayer
2. The golden number.
3. The day of the Paschal full moon.
4. The Sunday letter after the full moon.
5. Sticky-back plastic.
8. The Year of Our Lord.
9. Sharp knife *or* 500ml gin or other spirits.

Method:

First calculate your golden (or prime) number. To do this, add one to the Year of Our Lord, then divide by 19. The remainder is the golden number, unless there isn't a remainder, in which case the golden number is 19.

Next, add the Dominical, or Sunday letter (look in your Prayer Book for this). Calculate a quarter of the Year of our Lord, omitting fractions, and add this to the number of the Year of our Lord. Add the number 6.

Then divide the number by 7. Take away the number you first

thought of. If there is no remainder, then A is the Sunday letter. If there is a remainder, then the letter against that number in the small table (see your Prayer Book) is the Sunday letter. If you want to offset your last year's loss against income of an earlier year, enter the amount of the loss in box 3.28. Then look up the letter in the "Table to Find Easter Day".

Finally, check your result against the table in *The Alternative Service Book*. If you are wrong, you may *either* slit your wrists with a sharp knife (ask a grown-up to help you) *or* drink the gin or other spirits.

These things are sent to try us

"You make it July the 9th—Well your guess is as good as mine."

Every household has crises. There are a few that are highly specialized and relate only to vicarages, though. Running out of bread is a good example. Everyone finds that a nuisance. You go to make the children's packed lunches for school and there's only one crust of bread left. Even if you cut off the blue bits there's no way you're going to get two rounds of peanut butter sandwiches out of it. But picture the poor vicar. Flies back from taking school assembly, running a bit late for that home communion, dives towards bread bin and finds one crust of mouldy bread. Aargh! Have I got time to dash to the shop, or will a bit of judicious mould-shaving do the trick? After all, you only need a scrap. Will Herbert/Hilda notice, even? Or if I cut a circle out of an uncooked prawn cracker or poppadum, can I pass it off as a wafer? (I just made that last bit up, by the way. But you never know, it may come in handy for someone.)

The other main crises are bog-standard double booking incidents or simply forgetting things. Everyone does it occasionally, but there's more at stake when funerals are involved. Clergy have the mixed blessing of dealing with people at the major crisis points of their lives. For the poor old vicar there's nothing like wandering down the road to buy a paper and spotting a hearse pulling up outside your church. Even bungee-jumping won't give you an adrenalin buzz quite like it.

Vestments cause crises, too. I heard of a visiting cleric who was preaching on the text "Thou fool!" He opened his robes case to discover that instead of his surplice he'd packed a double bed sheet. My other favourite vestment story is of a theological college student who arrived late for a service. He dashed to the vestry with minutes to spare and to save time, only undid the top few buttons of his 39-button cassock and tried to dive inside. Unfortunately he was broad-shouldered and got stuck. He stood there wrestling and firing buttons around the vestry while the vicar hissed, "Next time don't be so flaming late!"

Saint of the week

HERETHRITH (9TH C), BISHOP AND MARTYR. FEAST: 27 FEBRUARY.

SECOND SUNDAY IN LENT

or
LENT 2
(Fifth Sunday before Easter)
(Violet [or Lent array])

═══════════════

These things are sent to try us

Callers at the vicarage are a well-known phenomenon to all clergy. Our present house doesn't actually look like a vicarage and it's a good mile away from the church. We only get one or two regulars who want sandwiches and a cup of tea. A year or so ago a violent alcoholic ex-convict used to drop by, but in the end I felt that I couldn't handle this and told him not to come back. He became a bit abusive and told me I wasn't as kind as the last people who lived here. "I only came because you've got a cross in the window!" he shouted. I'll soon move that, I thought.

I remember one occasion when we still lived in Gateshead and the boys were small. The doorbell rang while I was making their tea. It was someone wanting some food to tide him over till he could get his benefits sorted out. I gave him some and he went. Those are the bare bones of what happened, but the reality was much more complex. First of all the whole incident was punctuated with questions from my oldest son (then aged six), who was standing in his Power Ranger gear, which consisted of pyjamas, shin pads, Newcastle United back pack plus mask (pair of underpants on his head with his face looking out through a leghole). My three-year-old was in his "Morph" gear, which consists of being stark naked. This gave the episode a slightly odd feel.

"Who was it? What did he want? Is he very poor? I'm going to give him all my money," said the older one as I rummaged around trying to find tins, etc. "I've got 75p."

"We never give money," I said.

"Why not? Is it because he might spend it all on beer?"

"Sssh!"

There's nothing like trying to explain delicate things to small children for cutting through the waffle. We spend a lot of time telling them to be kind and generous. What are they supposed to think when they discover that there might be limits to our generosity?

I never cope well with people asking me for things at the door, or with beggars in the street. It feels like a choice between being mean or being taken for a ride. The little I give—is it to help the other person, or to salve my own conscience? I'm left feeling guilty because I have so much, but helpless because I don't know where my responsibility ends.

Guilt is only a hair's breadth away from resentment. And resentment soon finds reasons to justify itself. They're scroungers, a little voice whispers. If they're all thieves and bogus asylum seekers then it's not our problem. We no longer have to wrestle with our own helplessness, responsibility and fear.

Great church traditions

Going visiting

"Going visiting" is what vicars do. A fairly harmless occupation, you might think. But a few years back a clergyman near Birmingham was reported to the police by some over-zealous neighbours who saw him calling on an elderly parishioner. They pointed out that a dog collar could easily be used by conmen preying on pensioners.

Fortunately, it isn't easy to impersonate a vicar unless you're in the know. A few simple questions would soon smoke out an imposter. a) Where did you train? b) Has your PCC passed resolutions A, B and C? c) Under what circumstances should one seek alternative episcopal oversight? d) What is the date of the third Sunday in March? If your caller can answer all these questions without floundering, you've probably got the real Macoy on your doorstep, and, conveniently, the answer given to part b) will tell you whether to slam the door or not.

Saints of the week

BALDRED AND BILLFRITH (8TH C), NORTHUMBRIAN HERMITS.
FEAST: 6 MARCH.

THIRD SUNDAY IN LENT

or
LENT 3
(Fourth Sunday before Easter)
(Violet [or Lent array])

We have a Paschal candle in our porch at the moment. This isn't just the sad stump left over from last year, but a decent eighteen inches. There's a story behind this. A vicar I know bought a splendid brand-new candle for the church and put it proudly in its holder ready for Easter. Our church building is multi-purpose and one of the purposes is to host Ecumenical Lent lunches. Somebody decided that it was a bit nippy last Wednesday, so they turned on the overhead heaters. When the vicar came back an hour later to glance fondly at his candle two-thirds of it had melted away and formed a quite startling, free-standing abstract wax sculpture on the church floor. I say abstract, although a boatbuilder I know thought he could see the face of Christ in it. A new candle had to be swiftly ordered. There must be many of you reading this and trying to imagine a world in which church heaters are capable of taking the edge off the Arctic chill, let alone doing anything as dramatic as melting something. Here at St Paul's we have to consider these things. What about chocolate decorations on the church Christmas tree? Ought we to spray the bishop's mitre with flame-retardant? Unless it's Pentecost, of course.

These things are sent to try us

Church music—it comes in all kinds of forms from beautiful polyphonic motets in Norman cathedrals (yes, yes!) to the kind of chorus that functions like airport lounge music—to lull you into a false sense of security: "Ladies and gentlemen, please fasten your seatbelts. In a few moments this church is going to take off." (No, no!)

That's the big divide. Organ/choir versus music group. It's all down to personal taste. The important thing is that the music is done as well as possible, given the limitations/gifts of the congregation. It's NOT a theological issue, although great schisms in church history have taken place over lesser things than the disbanding of the robed choir. There can be few more bitter feuds than those between vicar and organist. Both believe that they are the trained professionals who know how the job of worship should be done.

There are many congregations who would respond to this wistfully. "If only we had an organist to feud with the vicar!" Which leads me to Roland. Is there a Roland in your life? Roland is an electronic keyboard who can play your hymns/choruses faultlessly for you, either in cathedral organ or in music group mode. Some of us miss the inimitable sound of hymnbook crashing onto keys, but that's just nostalgia. Interestingly, Roland also does sound effects, and if the mood takes you, you can substitute these noises for the pre-arranged accompaniment. My current favourite is "Be bold" to flushing loo and sub-machine-gun fire.

These are a few of my least favourite things

Housework

I hate tidying up after people. I hate hoovering and dusting. Clearly what I need is a cleaner. I was intrigued when a flyer came through our door advertising Nude Housecleaning to be undertaken by a male photographic model. Buffing in the buff. I should have kept it, because now nobody believes me. Sounds a bit dicey, though, nude housework. The thought of hoovering brings tears to the eyes. Or ironing. I had a friend who used to iron in her birthday suit and once burnt her bottom, don't ask me how. (Low board? Small kitchen? Big bottom?)

Typos of the week

HYMN SHEETS OFFER GREAT SCOPE FOR TYPOS,
AS DO OVERHEAD PROJECTOR ACETATES,
"CROWN HIM WITH MANY CROWS",
"WHOSE VICE IS CONTENTMENT, WHOSE PRESENCE IS BALM".

Saints of the week

FORTY MARTYRS OF SEBASTE (4TH C).
SOLDIERS WHO DIED OF EXPOSURE RATHER THAN RENOUNCE THEIR FAITH.
PATRONS OF NUDIST COLONIES (?) FEAST: 10 MARCH.

FOURTH SUNDAY IN LENT

or

LENT 4

(THIRD SUNDAY BEFORE EASTER)

MOTHERING SUNDAY

or

Refreshment Sunday

(Violet [or Lent array])

In the absence of Belgian chocolates, trips to Paris or IKEA vouchers, I was given a Mothering Sunday card from my older son with a tea bag stapled to it and a verse ending "But if you do get mad with me / Relax and have a cup of tea". Perhaps next year the card will be attached to a bottle of Gordons and the verse will read "But if I make a dreadful din / Relax and pour a nice stiff gin".

These things are sent to try us

My mother rang me recently to tell me about a piece she'd seen in *The Shropshire Star* about some research done on rats which demonstrated that motherhood increases brain power. This appears to contradict another bit of research I came across a while back which showed that you lose mental capacity during pregnancy. The latter, I'd have to say, is borne out by my own personal experience. Since having children my memory has been shot to pieces. So much so that I've occasionally wondered if I'm experiencing an early onset of senile thingummy, you know, that whatsit disease where you forget things all the time.

Now *The Shropshire Star* rats, after giving birth, apparently experienced an increase in brain activity which enabled them to be much better at solving puzzles which led to the discovery of food. They were much more alert in defending their litter against danger. That's all very fine and good, but what happened to the part of their brain which governs nouns, abstract thought, forward planning or reading books with more than forty pages? I bet nobody thought to test that. She may be infinitely ingenious at finding nourishment for her young, but when was the last time you overheard a mother rat deliver a cogent resumé of an opera plot?

If only the human brain was more like a computer. You could simply empty out all those useless things that clutter up the memory banks (the Donny Osmond's Birthday Syndrome) and make space for more important things. I would open a new file called "Days of the Week". "What day is it today?" I would ask myself. And I'd immediately know! Mind you, there have been times when I've been unable to recall which *decade* I'm in, so I must have clawed back a few brain cells from all that frenzied rat-like post-natal nurturing.

Great culinary disasters of our time

Simnel cake was traditionally a Mothering Sunday gift. I usually make one, but a vicar I know has gone off rich fruit cake. He suggested I might like to make a less rich one, "Like Liz's cakes". Pah! But after mature reflection I realized that I'd be making a net saving of one egg, a mouthful of brandy and about half a pound of dried fruit. This can go a long way in a frugal vicarage.

I made the cake on Saturday. Here's a hint (as Delia would say)— *don't* try to put a layer of marzipan in the middle of a cake like this. There simply is not enough fruit to support its weight and it will fall out through the wire rack as it cools. Your cake will sag in the middle. No! A "sad" sponge, as my grandma used to say. (She also used to refer to people "flapping about like Fanny Craddock's pastry".) The shame! Reach for that mouthful of brandy to steady your nerves. However, if this does happen, all is not lost. Simply scrape up the liquid marzipan with a fish slice and plaster it back into the cavity and leave to cool. That delicate lemony tang is achieved by the clever inclusion of a hint of Flash from the work surface.

Great church traditions

The eating of Judas

This festival coincides with the Festival of the Covering of the Simnel Cake. Cooks, discovering the difficulty in dividing a lump of marzipan into eleven equal balls resorted to making twelve instead, then eating Judas, the twelfth apostle.

Saint of the week

NICHOLAS OF FLUE (15TH C). SURPRISINGLY, THIS IS NOT SANTA CLAUS, BUT THE PATRON OF SWITZERLAND. FEAST: 21 MARCH.

PASSIONTIDE

FIFTH SUNDAY IN LENT

or
LENT 5
PASSION SUNDAY

(Second Sunday before Easter)
(Violet [or Lent array])

Just as you can recognize a vicarage even if the sign's been removed, there are ways of spotting off-duty clergy. For some species of cleric the most obvious marker is the sartorial colour scheme—a riot of black and grey. In the winter months you will start to see those furry Russian hats appearing, teamed with things like anoraks and plaid shopping trolleys. In the summer months you may spot that old clergy favourite, the shorts, sandal and beige ankle sock combo.

There are two objections to these observations. First, this kind of general weirdness could equally be Englishness. Secondly, not all clergy fit this stereotype. But you can still spot them. Take this example. Three young men in a tea shop. Clean-shaven, smartly dressed, squeaky clean, obviously professionals. So why aren't they in suits? Why are they wearing navy blue, fisherman rib chunky pullovers from Marks & Spencers? That's right—they're curates acting as assistant missioners at a university mission!

But what about women clergy? Can you spot them as easily out of uniform? The problem is spotting them *in* uniform, half the time. It's those very very pale shirts. Dog collars simply don't stand out against white. I'd have to do a bit of quiet eavesdropping before I could make a confident diagnosis. And like St Peter in the courtyard, it's your speech that betrays you most of all. Specialist terms like "the nunc" and "Graham Kendrick" and "to overconsecrate at the midnight" let the cat out of the bag straight away.

Addressing the clergy

Many people are under the impression that "Reverend" is a title, like Mrs or Dr. It's not, strictly speaking, any more than "Honorable" is. It's the Hon. *Stanley* Sidebottom, not Hon. Sidebottom. In the same way you aren't supposed to say Rev. Smith. It's Mr/Mrs/Ms/Dr Smith *or* Rev. Bert/ha Smith. If you don't believe me look in *Crockford's Clerical Directory*. There's a whole section on how to address a bishop. "The Rt Rev. Melvyn Fancy-Chasuble, Bishop of x"—yes. "Oi, you with the funny hat"—no. The correct form for an archbishop doesn't actually fit on a standard envelope (eg. "To the Most Reverend and Right Honorable Quietly Flamboyant By God's Grace His Urbane Shrewdness The Lord Archbishop of Dunstable").

Senior clergy have a hard life. Not only do they have to endure these strange archaic forms of address, they actually have to sign themselves in a peculiar way as well. Their surname vanishes and they get lumbered with the name of their diocese. Sometimes this is heavily disguised in Latin, eg. Dunelm, Cantuar, Ebor (which always makes me think "E-bor gum, missis!") Others end up with a moniker like "Dorking". There was an Anglo-Saxon bishop called Sexwulf, and I for one, would like to see this name reinstated; perhaps as a title bestowed on the winner of a Mr Universal Church contest.

If the good Lord had intended us to wear dog-collars, he would have given us little slots in our necks

Clergy get asked to all kinds of parties and it's frequently not clear whether they are on or off duty. Should you sport your dog collar or not? My handy hint is that if the venue is a club, go in mufti. A vicar I know was once mistaken for a strippergram. Being a vicar at a non-church party gets you into all kinds of interesting conversations. People pour out their worries and sorrows and vague religious aspirations. I used to think this was a knee-jerk reaction, rather like talking about cars to a mechanic. Now I've decided it's because most people never come into contact with "experts" in spiritual matters and are bowled over to find someone who deals in these categories all the time.

Saints of the week

GWYNLLYW AND GWLADYS (6TH C).
NOTED FOR THEIR ASCETICAL PRACTICE OF NUDE COLD-WATER BATHING IN THE USK. PATRON OF ANYONE FOOLISH ENOUGH TO SKINNY-DIP IN BRITISH COASTAL WATERS(?)
FEAST: 29 MARCH.

SIXTH SUNDAY IN LENT

or
PALM SUNDAY

(The Sunday next before Easter)
(Red)

———————————

When I was growing up, Palm Sunday in our Baptist church was "Egg and Flower Sunday". The children were all encouraged to bring along bunches of flowers and boxes of eggs and take them up to the front. It might equally well have been called "How to get egg yolk off the red carpet Sunday", as each year there was at least one accident. The eggs and flowers were later distributed among the elderly, housebound and deserving.

I don't remember any ritual involving palms, still less palm crosses (Papist nonsense). These are a standard part of Anglican life. I gather that you can buy palms and make your own crosses, but although I have often watched my sons dismantle their crosses, I have never known how to put them back together again. I can make paper aeroplanes, but that's as far as my origami skills go.

For me another problem is what to do with the cross afterwards. Pin it to the notice board? Stick it on the dashboard of the car? Compost it? Of course, if you are far enough up the candle you save them to burn next Ash Wednesday. Whatever you decide to do with them, you should never, as my sons do, use them for sword fights.

These things are sent to try us

Church magazines are very variable publications. I used to help edit one which was so dire that people used to plead with us to save trees instead. It was full of flower rotas and went out to every house in the parish, regardless of whether the occupants went to church. When we dropped all that and tried to make it sparky and relevant, people complained. There was a great deal of interest in who was doing the flowers in the church they never went to. I learnt a lot from that.

The other thing I learnt was that the most explosive, controversial topic known to British society is "dogs fouling footpaths". People get far more violent on this subject than on politics, homelessness, Europe and the Toronto blessing rolled into one.

Ordinary parish mags tend to have certain features in common. The cover consists of a drawing of the church building which is usually photocopied onto a different colour of paper each month to save confusion and spare you from accidentally reading it twice. Inside you will find a letter from the vicar/rector who probably thought, "Oh no," just before writing it. There will be typos, eg. "Evensnog". There may be adverts: "Volunteers needed, to hell with the fête." You may also find a section called "From the Registers". This will be a list of baptisms, weddings and funerals and it may look straightforward, but it's up there with dogs and pavements for its explosive potential. If you don't believe me, try mis-spelling the deceased's name, some time.

Saint of the week

MADRUN (5TH C). PATRON OF MARATHON COMPETITORS (?)
FEAST: 9 APRIL.

MAUNDY THURSDAY

(Red, or as in Lent:
White at Holy Communion)

This is the day which commemorates Christ washing his disciples' feet. It is re-enacted in some churches, though others, balking perhaps at the thought of bunions and verrucas, have a hand-washing ceremony instead. This smacks a bit of Pontius Pilate to me. The Queen traditionally distributes Maundy money to deserving cases on this day. I imagine this tradition grew up because, frankly, there is little one would not pay to be let off washing one's subjects' feet.

In other places the ceremony of the Blessing of the Oils (White) takes place. The oils are then distributed in little bottles labelled "Oil for the Sick". I once ended up walking gloomily round the streets of Lichfield in the rain with my two small sons while this was going on, having decided that the service would be too much for them. We arranged to meet a vicar I know outside the main doors. When the service was due to end I sat with the boys and other outcasts, huddled in the rain. From inside we could hear the faint and muffled sounds of the service. Then a hymn struck up. It got gradually louder and louder as the procession came down the aisle towards us. Suddenly we heard the sound of the great doors opening. Light, warmth and music flooded gloriously out and the whole congregation, bishops and all, poured forth to meet us in the rain.

What a good image of heaven, I thought. Present all the time, dimly perceived as we sit in the rain, then finally bursting out with great joy to meet us.

GOOD FRIDAY

(Red, hangings removed)

A few years ago, one of the supermarket chains ran a campaign saying "Chocolate—the true meaning of Easter". I'm convinced that this is true for most people in Britain. If you pin them down most will remember that Easter is to do with the resurrection of Christ, but in practical terms it's more about Bank Holidays and confectionery. Easter eggs are about as pagan as you can get, celebrating as they do the Germanic goddess Eostre, but it would be hard to summon the energy to campaign against them—especially if you've just given chocolate up for Lent.

Chocolate is the acceptable face of Passiontide. Eggs and bunnies, yes. Death and resurrection, no thanks. The church quite rightly seeks to challenge this with marches of witness on Good Friday. The effectiveness of these events varies. In the town where I grew up we used to get funny looks from the shoppers as we had our ecumenical open-air worship. I've been to another march of witness which avoided this embarrassment altogether by setting off in the early evening after the shops had shut.

Here in Walsall the march passes straight through the crowded market, to the annoyance of shoppers and traders alike. The marchers get in the way. They disrupt things for, ooh, several minutes at a time. Comments get hurled, some of which are worth treasuring: "It's disgusting! And on Good Friday, too!" At the front of the march there are people in costume taking the role of Jesus, the soldiers and so on, and there is a stark cross. One year someone complained that it "frightens the children". This is something the Easter bunny has yet to be accused of.

It's tempting to sigh at the way the gospel has been watered down, but even in church we tend to tame the events of Good Friday. A vicar I know once produced a crutch as a sermon illustration and asked what it was for. "To lean on, to support you if you've broken your leg, to help you walk," came the reply. He then produced a large cross and asked the same question. "To lean on," people said. "To offer support, to help you get through life." Eventually I said, "It's for killing people." To my astonishment everyone laughed. The cross had become a symbol of comfort, not an instrument of torture and execution.

Vicarage children

This year my older son got the role of Jesus in his school's Easter production. He was clearly honoured, but aware of other children saying, "You only got that part because your Dad's a vicar." I'm sure it has as much to do with his photographic memory. He learns not only his own part, but the entire script, and can remember every word I have ever uttered, in order to bring it up in evidence and use against me at some later date. The trickiest part, of course, is when Judas has to kiss him—which is deeply no-no for nine-year-old boys. "Do people say you're gay?" I asked. "One person did," he replied. "But I threatened to hit him round the head with my cross in the next scene, so he stopped." I'm still unpacking the theological implications of that.

"Look, just wipe the blood off, Judas; now shake hands and say 'sorry', both of you."

SEASON
OF
EASTER

EASTER SUNDAY

Resurrection of the Lord
or
EASTER 1
(unless other provision is made)
(White or Gold)

This joyful Eastertide, away with sin and sorrow!
My love, the crucified, hath sprung to life this morrow.
Had Christ, who once was slain, ne'er burst his three-day
prison,
Our faith had been in vain, but now is Christ arisen,
Arisen, arisen, arisen!

This is my favourite Easter hymn. Both the words and the tune capture something of the wild joy and total strangeness of the resurrection. What saddens me is that this is so seldom glimpsed in your average Evangelical Easter Day sermon. I think this is because we Evangelicals are such resolute "empty-tombers" that we tend to think that what I call the "Easter forensic sermon" is the only way to convince people of the truth of our claims. If only we can demonstrate in an imaginary court of law that the tomb was *genuinely* empty, the body not stolen by disciples but *genuinely* raised by God, then everyone will throw up their hands in surrender and come to faith.

To me this kind of approach feels a bit brow-beating, a kind of intellectual bullying of the sort I occasionally associate with C S Lewis. Oops! Accidental heresy. No doubt I shall be made to apologize to him if we meet in glory. The problem is that I find it so totally alien from the risen Christ of the Gospels. Preach on the Emmaus Road, preach on Mary at the tomb and leave forensics alone for once.

Liturgical blunders

I was once visiting a church on Easter Day and the vicar came in and pronounced in ringing tones, "He is not risen! He is here!" and all the congregation—apart from me—responded joyously, "Hallelujah!" A moment later I began to think I had imagined it. I have also seen that text quoted correctly on a communion table in some seriously hot prot church. Unfortunately, the only bit you could read as you came up for communion were the words, "He is not here here." The words "Then why are we bothering?" kind of sprang to mind.

Vicarage children

From a very early age vicarage children know all the answers in assemblies and children's addresses. I have sat with my older son listening to an address about football teams and heard him mutter with heavy sarcasm, "But on *Jesus'* team we can *all* take part, no matter how good or bad we are!" getting in just before the preacher said it.

Once, when my younger son was only two he called me a silly bugger. When I enquired gently where he'd heard that word, he replied, "On Thomas the Tank engine." Not entirely satisfied with this answer, I asked if anyone had called him it. "Yes." "Who?" "Jesus." There you are—every vicarage child knows that when in doubt, there's a sporting chance "Jesus" is the right answer.

Saint of the week

MAELRUBBA (7TH–8TH C), MONK AND APOSTLE OF THE PICTS. FEAST: 21 APRIL.

"Mummy, I think Jesus has been at the chocolate biscuits again."

SECOND SUNDAY OF EASTER

or

THE FIRST SUNDAY AFTER EASTER

or

EASTER 2
Low Sunday
(White)

—————————

By now most of us have lapsed back into our pre-Lenten sloth and gluttony. Before long, though, we will have to begin projecting into the future and imagining how we will look in our swimsuits in July if we carry on at this rate. We will even go so far as to contemplate enrolling for a fitness class. But beware! I read once in a *Which?* report that fitness centres can be bad for you. I'd suspected it all along. The real cause for concern, whether in private or in public clubs, was the low level of instruction in aerobic classes. I read all this with keen interest, as I have been known to go in for a spot of keep fit myself.

I can still remember the leaflet produced by the local leisure centre when we lived in Gateshead. "Keep fit the fun way." Well, that's a lie for a start. There *is* no fun way of keeping fit. That's like saying, "Expilation." I say all this from a female perspective. Men do team things to keep fit, and this may be fun, for all I know. For women, though, keep fit is a solitary and miserable thing; penance for all those times they've eaten a whole pack of Penguin bars, hidden the wrapper, gone out and bought another pack, then eaten just one and put the rest in the cupboard.

Take your average steps aerobics class. The first problem is what to wear. In Gateshead, when I went in for such things, lycra was compulsory. To begin with, from my vantage point (ie, skulking at the back) it didn't look too bad. Lots of other people seemed to be wearing leggings and baggy T-shirts. Then the instructor appeared and everyone else whipped off their baggy T-shirts to reveal cropped sports tops and thong leotards. Thongs! Have they no shame? Have they no haemorrhoids?

Then the music started and it was warm-up time. That was usually enough for me, but because I was at the back I couldn't sneak out unnoticed. I was trapped for the next fifty minutes with a room full of women going, "Step jump! Step jump!" while I was somehow locked in a pattern of going, "Jump step! Jump step!" and unable to break out of it. I floundered on till the stomach exercises. At least these offered a welcome opportunity to lie on the floor. This is when you had the time to notice properly what you'd feared was there all along—a row of men perving in the gallery because nobody remembered to shut the curtains. Maybe that's the "fun" element.

Afterwards I staggered back to my car, only to find my leg was too weak to work the clutch. Why do it? Why pay good money to humiliate and half-kill yourself? Maybe it's short-term memory loss. You forget each time just how bad it is. And how unbiblical! Doesn't the psalmist say, "My soul delights itself in fatness"?

Vicarage children

If you are clergy it's compulsory to give your children biblical names. Here is the list you must choose from: *Boys:* Jonathan, Joshua, Joseph, Thomas, James, Barnabas. *Girls:* Rebecca, Jemima, Hannah, Anna, Ruth, Bethany. There is another constraint. You want your children to talk to you when they are older, so here are some names to avoid: *Boys:* Ham, Mash, Zerubbabel. *Girls:* Keren-happuch.

Let's face it—your kids will be peculiar enough without the handicap of a silly name.

When they get bigger they will have to develop ways of coping. Some of these won't be pleasant. In the States there's a recognized condition called PK (Preacher's Kid) Syndrome. Basically, when everyone is expecting you to be a goody-goody, it's very difficult not to rebel. What hope is there for me? Not only am I a PK, I'm also a PW.

Saint of the week

EGBERT (8TH C), MONK AND BISHOP. FEAST: 24 APRIL.

THIRD SUNDAY OF EASTER

or

THE SECOND SUNDAY AFTER EASTER

or

EASTER 3

(Use of controls, adjustments or procedures not listed in this manual may result in hazardous radiation exposure)

(White)

The vicar's letter in the parish magazine. This may seem like a totally harmless mundane task in a vicar's life. Beware. You might, for example, write what you consider to be a standard vicarly grumble about the over-commercialization of Christmas, confiding in your parishioners that you don't like Christmas that much, and going on to say how good it would be if we focused on the true meaning of the incarnation. Not very sparky, perhaps, but it's only going to be read by the flock. Wrong! What you don't realize is that there's someone at your local gazette or chronicle office whose job it is to read all the local church magazines and look for stories. Before you know what's hit you, there's a headline in your local rag saying, "Why I Hate Christmas." You splutter in indignation, That's not what I said! Then you calm down and tell yourself, "Oh well, nobody reads *The Chronicle*." Wrong again! There's someone sitting in a regional press agency whose job it is to read local papers. They ring you up and sound like rational sympathetic human beings. You explain what you actually meant and hang up, relieved that you've had a chance to set the record straight. The next morning there will be headlines in the tabloids: "BAN CHRISTMAS SAYS REV. SCROOGE!" And your phone will ring non-stop with requests for interviews and pleas for you to appear on TV panels. My hot tip is put the answer machine on and lie low. It'll blow over. As a wise Franciscan once said to me, "It's like the tide. It *will* go out again."

Two more things to remember: August is the silly season. Stories that would not normally be given a moment's attention suddenly become hot news items. Secondly, think carefully before you give an opinion to your local paper on some trivial-seeming matter. A vicar I know was rung up by a journalist for his reaction to the news that planning permission was being sought to open a lap-dancing club just round the corner from his church. He wisely declined to comment until the permission went through. You can imagine how it would go. Vicar trying to tread that tricky line of loving the sinner, etc. and saying something bland like, "Well, of course, if any of the young ladies concerned came to our Sunday service I hope we'd make them welcome," only to see the headlines scream: "VICAR WELCOMES LAP DANCERS!" The best answer he came up with in the end was "I'm all in favour of encouraging folk-dancing, be it from Lapland or anywhere else."

Liturgical blunders

I once heard a story which perfectly illustrates the clash between low and high church. An Evangelical was invited to preach at an Anglo-Catholic church. He processed in behind the high-church vicar, who was doing his usual thing of keeping his eyes piously fixed on a remote spot in the middle distance. The Evangelical, as was his custom, was looking from side to side, smiling and making eye contact with the congregation as he passed down the aisle. Unfortunately, he didn't notice that the vicar had paused in front of the altar to genuflect deeply. The Evangelical promptly tripped over him and somersaulted into the chancel. The highchurchman got up, hissed, "You ass!" and carried on as though nothing had happened.

Dr Spooner's fun spot

I come from a family which continues Dr Spooner's splendid tradition of wuddling up mords. The best are those which happen accidentally, especially from the pulpit. "They shall mount up on ings like weagles", or "It is easier for a camel to go through the knee of an idol" are two good examples of the genre.

Saint of the week

ERKENWALD (7TH C), BISHOP OF LONDON. FEAST: 30 APRIL.

FOURTH SUNDAY OF EASTER

or

THE THIRD SUNDAY AFTER EASTER

or

EASTER 4

(White)

Like many small-time hypochondriacs, I scour the health pages of my newspaper and scare myself silly about things like pigeon dung and vitamin supplements. In fact, I think that health pages should carry their own health warning: "Some readers may find the information contained in this article distressing." Of course, this would completely misfire, because if I read that I'd immediately think, "What? What? They're trying to hide something from me!"

And if this isn't enough, you can now buy entire magazines devoted to giving yourself sleepless nights. Those of us suffering from a morbid turn of mind should avoid health and fitness publications at all costs, even if there is

"Don't worry about measles Mrs Jones, it's just blackcurrant juice splashes."

nothing else to read in the dentist's waiting room except yachting magazines from the mid-seventies. But how can you tell in advance if you are the kind of person who's susceptible to hypochondria? Here's a simple test. You wake up one morning and find you have a mouth ulcer. How much time elapses before you wonder if it might be cancer of the tongue? a) one nano second b) half an hour c) it wouldn't cross your mind unless you were reading this rubbish. As and Bs should stick to yachting magazines.

These are a few of my least favourite things

Manmade fibres

I suspect that somewhere there is a sinister group trying to force a man-made fibre come-back. I keep reading bits of research that tell us the safest thing to wear in the sun is dark-coloured polyester. I also read about a new breed of super-housemite fast invading the homes of southern England, where our lovely wool carpets are guaranteeing them a warm welcome. These mites cause asthma attacks. Well, I suppose that the dangers of asthma outweigh the risk of accidentally electrocuting yourself while sliding down your nylon stair carpet in a pair of navy crimplene slacks.

Some artificial fibres are trendy at the moment. Tencel, for instance; and another one which momentarily escapes me, but sounds something like cuprinol. Aren't these just new ways of wearing nylon without having to go out and shoot yourself? But nylon can be fun. I can remember wearing a brushed nylon nightie between brushed nylon sheets as a child. If you wriggled vigorously, you could have your very own private firework display under the covers. It occurs to me now that adults in the sixties must have had a crackling good time in this department. "You set my lips on fire" takes on a whole new meaning.

Favourite health scares

GM food

The great GM food debate rumbles ever on. I can remember when *The Times* revealed that the traditional English lettuce is being targeted for modification. "British and Italian researchers," says the report, "have found a way to make lettuces curlier, crunchier, faster growing and less likely to wilt." This is a bit like trying to make the British sausage non-greasy, rusk-free and not stuffed with puréed pig toe-nails—in other words, totally unlike itself.

Maybe I should be grateful for any advance which makes the eating of vegetables less of a chore and more of a delight. I have a friend in the States, a real right-on wholefood hippy type, who shops each week for her organic veg. and carries them home and up three flights of stairs and puts them in her fridge. Two weeks later, when they are rotten, she carries them back down three flights of stairs and puts them out with the trash. It eventually dawned on her that she could save herself the stairs and put the veg straight in the bin on the way home from the shops.

If this is how an American wholefood hippy acts, what hope is there for the likes of me? Or my children? If the GM brigade want to do something really useful they can modify peas so that they look and taste like a bag of M&Ms.

Saint of the week

WIRO (8TH C), MONK AND BISHOP OF UTRECHT
FEAST: 8 MAY.

FIFTH SUNDAY OF EASTER

or
THE FOURTH SUNDAY AFTER EASTER
or
EASTER 5
(White)

Favourite health scares

Headlice

Those of you who have school-age children will already be aware of this health scare. We're facing a plague; a new super breed of headlice, fast becoming resistant to the sheep-dip fluid we all happily doused our children in until we were told oops! sorry, it's actually carcinogenic. I'm now going to embark on an in-depth description of nits, so you may like to avert your gaze.

You get quite blasé about lice after a while. I once had an anguished phone call from another mother. It was clear she was trying to broach some incredibly difficult and sensitive issue. I began to fear that my son had been bullying hers and was mightily relieved to discover it was nothing more than nits. In fact, it can all get rather competitive. Nits? Pah! I see your nits and I raise you threadworms and impetigo! There really isn't the same stigma attached to parasites nowadays. We all know that head lice *prefer clean hair*. This is what we mums assure one another as our darlings are infested yet again. Unfortunately children are quick to spot the logical solution to the problem—never wash your hair.

However, no matter what we say, we still believe at some

primitive level that lousy = filthy. I discovered some creepy crawlies in my sons' hair while we were on holiday and went to a chemist and asked discreetly for a fine comb (technical term). I was offered an ordinary comb.

"This is the finest we've got."

"Oh. I wanted it for um," (drops voice) *"head lice...."*

"Oh a NIT comb, you mean," bawled the chemist. "Here you are."

At the moment we're not supposed to be using the nit shampoo. This is what you do instead. First, fell the child with a rugby tackle while their hair's wet from the bath. Then get a half-nelson on them before attempting futilely to comb each individual hair to remove any lice/eggs while the child screams and squirms. Threats/bribes may be used at any stage. I must admit there is a certain satisfaction in combing out a live one. "Aha!" you shout triumphantly. "They can run, but they can't hide!" Or more accurately, they can hide but they can't run. After a week of this most parents crack and break open an illicit bottle of carbaryl, hoping nobody will smell it.

One interesting thing, though, before I leave this subject for ever. Men seem to be afflicted with some kind of congenital blindness on this matter. Once I became obsessed with the idea that I'd got them, and every so often I'd ask a vicar I know to check for me. He'd finger my hair for approximately half a second and say, "Nope. Can't see any," before returning to the next gripping episode of Ceefax, or whatever he was doing. It wasn't till I went swimming and felt them scuttling that I knew he was wrong.

Dr Spooner's fun spot

One thing we were never supposed to do as children was to Spoonerize choruses. This came under the heading of "Making mock of hymns". Of course, this made it twice as funny. "As with madness Glen of old" was one of our favourites, along with "We plough the scields and fatter", "Shoving lephard of thy sheep" and "Bust and otrey".

Saint of the week

PRUDENTIANA (1ST–2ND C), SUPPOSED ROMAN MARTYR. FEAST: 19 MAY.

SIXTH SUNDAY OF EASTER

or

THE FIFTH SUNDAY AFTER EASTER

or

EASTER 6

(Rogationtide, being the Monday, Tuesday
and Wednesday before Holy Thursday,
or The Ascension of our Lord)
(To store any changes,
press the green button)

(White)

These are a few of my least favourite things

Moving house

Since marrying a vicar I know some seventeen years ago we have moved house six times. This is not unusual in clergy circles. Outsiders often comment on it and ask me whether we have to move on every few years. My heart sinks and I'm tempted to say "Yes" and have done with it. It's hopeless trying to explain to outsiders how the church works. They usually want to compare it either with the armed forces with the bishop posting clergy about; or they try to understand it in terms of career progression. "So you're a team vicar now and you're going to be priest-in-charge. Is that a step up?"

When you're a curate, moving on is normally straightforward. You do three years and then you go. What they never teach you at theological college is the art of breaking it to the congregation you are leaving. It's the ecclesiastical equivalent of a "Dear John" letter. You can't avoid phrases like "There's no easy way of putting this" or "The time has come for us to move on". If you aren't careful you end up blurting out, "But I hope we can always be friends!"

Another word of caution. Think carefully about the *name* of the place you're going to. When we were moving to Walsall from Gateshead a lot of people wondered why we felt called to Poland. Another vicar I know went to a place called Hebburn. "Oh dear," said a shocked parishioner. "Was that very sudden?"

I hate moving house, but it's been such a recurring feature of my adult life that I almost take it for granted, though. I forget that for other people moving from one end of the country to the other is unimaginable. It comes as a surprise to me when I ask someone, "Have you always lived here?" and they reply, "Ooh, no! I used to live on Myrtle Road."

My way of coping is to focus on the new house. The planning stage is very rewarding. You can redecorate the entire place from top to bottom without shifting from your chair. The only problem is that I create these elaborate schemes in the privacy of my own brain and fail to communicate them to a vicar I know. He makes some mild suggestion about putting the armchairs in the sitting room and I recoil with horror. "But the sitting room is duck egg blue with shades of minted lavendar! We can't put the armchairs in that colour scheme— unless we have loose covers made. Aha! We could get them done in unbleached linen union to match the curtains, of course. Good. That's settled, then." Being a sensible man he usually lets me get on with it on the grounds that if *I'm* happy, *his* life will be nicer. And anyway, if he says nothing I may change my mind and go down the mulberry route in a couple of days, in which case the armchairs will be *perfect* as they are.

Colour schemes are a form of escapism. I can plot my emotional state quite accurately by the number of interior design magazines I buy. They're a bit pricey, but it's a cheaper habit than booze or cigarettes.

Liturgical blunders

A vicar I know needed to print some funeral orders of service. He decided that the simplest thing was to use one from the previous funeral (for a man named John) and use the "find and exchange" mechanism on his computer. He did this, then ran off forty copies, only to notice that "I am the resurrection and the life" was now from Tommy 11 v. 25.

"Me too, Bob—still, a dab of turtlewax brings it up lovely."

Saint of the week

BOBOLA (1591–1657), POLISH MARTYR. FEAST: 21 MAY.

ASCENSION DAY

(Fortieth Day, Sixth Thursday after Easter)

(From Friday after Ascension Day
begin the nine days of prayer
before Pentecost)

(White or Gold)

In my nonconformist youth both Ascension Day and Pentecost always seemed like glamorous and faintly Papist-sounding festivals. I was also confused in my third-year German class when Lieselotte and Hans were celebrating something called *"Maria Himmelfahrt"* I thought "Eh? I don't remember *that* from the Bible."

These days we refer to that as the Feast of the Massive Assumption, despite (or, possibly, because of) the fact that one of my sisters and her husband have Gone Over to Rome. This has been accepted in good part by my nonconformist parents. I like to think I paved the way by marrying an Anglican, then becoming one myself. Shortly after my sister's defection (I'm sure the Roman Church has a different word for it), my mother used to wake at three in the morning and think, "But what about the Reformation? What was that all about, then?" But we all seem to have ridden the ecclesiastical storm and are all still talking to one another. I used to think that owning up to being an Evangelical was hard, but according to my brother-in-law, that's nothing compared with admitting you've just become a Roman Catholic. He said people looked at him as though he'd just announced he'd joined the Khmer Rouge.

Ascension and Pentecost are marked in many Anglican churches by the annual challenge of trying to work out the tune for "Hail thee festival day" and feeling there should be more to it, somehow, than there usually is. Pentecost tends to come into its own in more charismatically-inclined congregations, but Ascension Day still leaves most of us faintly stumped. This year was the first time that the significance of a line from Wesley's "Hail the day that sees him rise" really struck me: "He the first-fruits of our race". Christ was one of our own, one of *us*, a local lad made cosmically good. Think back, if you can bear to, to the year Man U did the treble, and picture the scenes in the streets of Manchester when the team paraded their trophies. This is the palest shadow of the welcome Christ received:

> There for him high triumph waits.
> Lift your heads, eternal gates.
> He hath conquered death and sin,
> Let the King of glory in: Alleluia!

Liturgical blunders

When a vicar I know was at theological college he was part of "The Federation", which sounds thrillingly like a brewery, but is in fact only the name for the group of theological colleges in Cambridge. One Ascension Day the high-church Anglicans held an outdoor eucharist, which had its exciting moments. Would the altar cross fall over? Yes... No... Yes! Down it came, in a great scything motion behind the acolyte. This was the first time I'd ever seen cassock albs and I found them faintly Klannish. At the far side of the quad there was a small but persistent voice going, "But I have to go *now*, Mummy. I have to go NOW." The best part was the brilliant idea of letting off fireworks at the end of the service; but all great liturgical ideas are only as good as the operators. The wrong signal was given and the entire post-communion prayer was punctuated by alarming whizzes and bangs.

SEVENTH SUNDAY OF EASTER

or

THE SIXTH SUNDAY AFTER EASTER

or

THE SUNDAY AFTER ASCENSION DAY
(Easter 6)
(The Visit of the Blessed Virgin Mary
to Elizabeth may be celebrated on
2 July instead of 31 May)

(White)

"Quinquennial" is one of those deeply ecclesiastical words like "sexagesima" or "Hnngraargh oof!" (the sound of a vicar stumbling over a hassock during a power cut) which is next to meaningless outside church circles. The quinquennial is an archaic ritual which comes round every five years, when the church fabric is examined to determine whether the steeple is about to topple off onto little old ladies passing below, or if the sexton is infested with deathwatch beetles.

There is also an annual archdeacon's visitation, where in the olden days the vicar and churchwardens assemble at church and try to round up and count the hymnbooks, chalices, etc. Sometimes they wear powerful aftershave, hoping that this will detract from the smell of fresh paint and the visiting archdeacon won't notice they've redecorated the chancel without a faculty. (A faculty is a technical Anglican term for the retrospective permission sought from the diocese after work has been done.) Increasingly, archdeacons are conducting an Inventory of Mission. This is all part of the sea change in which churches must move from "maintenance to missionary mode", or perish.

Quinquennials are also done on vicarages. I believe these are conducted by diocesan surveyors, but I wouldn't be surprised if the archdeacon came too. Every room in the house is inspected. Wonky doors, etc. are noted. You *can* try making suggestions: "The kitchen lino's a bit worn. What about antique Provençal quarry tiles?" Realistically, however, the best you can hope for is to choose the colour of the new lino. Dirt brown is my hot tip. The system of inspection, though threatening, does ensure that vicarages are tidied on a regular five-year basis. This doesn't extend as far as vicarage cupboards, of course. Before opening any cupboard the sensible archdeacon will insure himself against accidental death under a cascade of 1970s Christian paperbacks and broken dartboards.

Great church traditions

Churchwardens

The main function of churchwardens is to be kind to the vicar. They can make all the difference between a parish being bearable or not. When they are appointed, wardens have to go to a grand swearing-in with the archdeacon. This conjures up a wonderful picture—a roomful of otherwise respectable church folk turning the air blue. The archdeacon does the Archdeacon's Charge, which also sounds intriguing. I've never been privileged to hear one, but I imagine it goes something like this:

> Half a league, half a league,
> Half a league onward,
> Canon to right of them,
> Canon to left of them,
> Canon in front of them,
> Volleyed and thundered.
> Someone had blundered!

> Theirs not to make reply
> Theirs not to reason why,
> Theirs but to do and die.
> Into the valley of Death
> Rode the Churchwardens!

Actually, I'm sure it's not *that* bad, if you're thinking of standing at the next AGM.

Vicarage children

Vicarage children, when they are small, don't realize that they come from a weird family. Home is normal to them. They copy Mum and Dad, the way all small children do. They find little bits of bread, cheese quavers, or polystyrene packaging chips, snap them in half and offer them to bemused visitors with the words "The body of Christ". They arrange all the little chairs in the house into a circle, put a sheet of paper on each and play "meetings" (fun fun fun!).

Saint of the week

GUDWAL (6TH C), OBSCURE CELTIC ABBOT. FEAST: 6 JUNE.

DAY OF PENTECOST

or

PENTECOST
(Whit Sunday)

or

WHITSUNDAY
(Ember Days: Wednesday, Friday and
Saturday after the Feast of Pentecost)

(Red)

═══════════════

In the olden days nobody talked about Pentecost. It was always "Whitsunday" and the half-term holiday was "Whitsun". Sadly, this is dying out and becoming "May bank holiday", which is a shame, and confusing, as there are two May bank holidays. My dictionary tells me that the Old English *hwita sunnendaeg*, white Sunday, was "probably named after the ancient custom of wearing white robes at or after baptism". Pentecost is a red Sunday, instead, another change I feel vaguely sad about. Personally, I blame it on the EU.

Liturgical blunders

We had a pigeon problem in church this weekend. Two got in through an open window on Friday night and resisted all attempts of eviction. We baulked at the idea of putting down poisoned food, partly because it might result in some unfortunate imagery on Pentecost Sunday: "The Holy Spirit descended on them from above like a dead pigeon from the rafters, thunk!" It doesn't capture the mood, somehow.

(Animal lovers will be pleased to hear that the birds found their own way out, unharmed.)

These are a few of my least favourite things

Pigeons

Mary Poppins has a lot to answer for. "Feed the birds, tuppence a bag." Why, *why* do people feed urban pigeons? Do they think that otherwise they will starve? One look into their wily eyes will tell you that here is a creature adapted for survival. The fact that they have grown fat and stupid on a diet of two loaves of mighty white per bird per day shouldn't mislead us. The pigeon is a dangerous creature. It's their status as birds that protects them. We don't indulge in such sentimentality when it comes to rodents. "Feed the rats, tuppence a bag" doesn't have the same ring to it. And that's all pigeons are—rats on wings. They spread disease and they destroy the environment. I say this with some feeling. Our old church in Gateshead faced a bill of some £75,000 to restore the west front damaged, at least in part, by acidic pigeon dung.

Helpful hints from the vicar's wife

What to do on Pentecost Sunday

"Let's go fly a kite!" This seems to me to be an eminently suitable Whitsun activity, tapping into the seasonal wind/spirit imagery. Having said that, our own family kite-flying expeditions haven't always been totally successful, but no doubt there's a sermon illustration in there somewhere.

I can remember the occasion when my sons bought a kite each from Harry Tuffin's Pound Shop near my parents' house. In fact, some of my friends are probably under the impression my maiden name was Tuffin, as the boys always say, "We're going to see Grandma and Harry Tuffin." We tried to fly these kites on the hill above Knighton, but what do you expect for a pound? They looked quite impressive, each sporting an eagle (named, mysteriously, Paul and Derek by our younger son), but they never entirely got airborne—unless you count dropping them over the bannisters onto grandparents passing in the hall below.

Later we acquired two amazing "pocket kites". We tried them on the South Downs, springing jauntily from cowpat to cowpat. This is one of the hazards of kite-flying not mentioned by Mary Poppins, or more properly, Merry Parpuns. If you're looking up you can't see what you're treading in. That also sounds like a sermon illustration of something, but I can't think what.

Saint of the week

DOGMAEL (6TH C), WELSH MONK.
INVOKED TO HELP CHILDREN LEARN TO WALK.
FEAST: 14 JUNE.

"*I bet Mary Poppins wouldn't fly half so high if she had some of this muck on her practically perfect turned out toes!*"

ORDINARY TIME

TRINITY SUNDAY

or
PENTECOST 1

(The Thursday after Trinity Sunday
may be observed as a day of
Thanksgiving for the Institution of
Holy Communion, [Corpus Christi])

(White or Gold on Sunday;
Green from Monday)

(Seven for the seven stars in the sky)

Trinity Sunday is the day when those of us who have previously encountered the hymn "I bind unto myself today" get a good laugh at the expense of everyone else when the tune changes wildly and unpredictably to something else half way through. Just when they've got the hang of the new tune, it goes back to the old one again. We might also get the added thrill of singing "Consubstantial, co-eternal, while unending ages run" and wondering what this could mean.

If Trinity falls on the first (or third) Sunday of the month, it might coincide with All Age Worship. We call it All Age, but in reality, most older people stay away, either because They Want Their Communion, or because they don't like loud hymns or being bashed on the head with a toy car by the toddler sitting behind them—all excellent reasons in their way. The person doing the children's address will produce a kettle, an ice-cube and a glass of water to illustrate the three-in-one nature of the Trinity. Alternatively, he or she might explode an egg in a microwave, eat a daffodil (or a tin of dogfood), catch a ping-pong ball on their nose or juggle kitchen knives while fire-eating. Afterwards, nobody will remember quite how this illustrates the Trinity, but they will all agree that it was a jolly good service.

Liturgical blunders

I once knew of a Baptist minister who had an unhappy time at one particular church. In the end he decided to move on, but felt led to pray to the Lord that he might "end his ministry there in a blaze of glory". That night there was a fire in the church.

Sometimes it's difficult to know how to interpret signs of this kind. I well remember when York Minster was struck by lightning shortly after the consecration of David Jenkins as Bishop. Many interpreted it as a sign of divine wrath; but this leaves us with a bit of a problem with divine timing, doesn't it? I can also remember reading of another lightning strike which burnt out the scrambling device on a porn channel, with the result that up and down the country people could suddenly see adult movies for free. What was God trying to say *there*, I wonder? Or was that the devil?

"No Mother, that's not Harry Secombe and you are NOT phoning the BBC for that club's website!"

Handy hints from the vicar's wife

Bringing up boys

If you have small boys, why not consider a Call to the Inner City? There are always lots of fire engines to wave at. When we lived in Gateshead we used to hear them tearing along the roads all through the night. On occasion we called them out ourselves when other small boys set fire to the wasteland at the back of the house in high summer. That certainly livened up a boring afternoon towards the end of the six weeks' holiday. Once there was an engine in the local park and children were allowed to climb into the cab and try the sirens.

"It's got seven horns," explained the fireman.

"Aha! Like the Beast of the Apocalypse, you mean," said a vicar I know. The fireman looked at him very strangely indeed, for all I know wondering why a vicar didn't remember that the Beast had ten horns and seven heads.

Saint of the week

TRILLO (?5TH C), ABBOT. FEAST: 15 JUNE.

SECOND SUNDAY AFTER PENTECOST

or

FIRST SUNDAY AFTER TRINITY

or

PENTECOST 2

(Trinity 1)

[Proper 4]

(Unless you are allergic to shellfish)

(Green)

―――――――――――

once watched a TV programme devoted to examples of bad driving. I found it reassuring to know that there are many drivers out there so much more incompetent than I am. I have never, for instance, driven into wet concrete, or gone the wrong way down the motorway. Neither have I driven at 110mph with only three wheels on the car ("You know, I *thought* the handling was a bit peculiar, officer...").

It might be quite nice to do something so flamboyant. All my motoring fiascos have been of a rather girlie nature and have taken place at speeds of under 3mph and involved boring things like gateposts and stupidly-placed walls. I find it a bit depressing to conform so obviously to gender stereotyping. Even if I had a really fast flash motor I'm sure I'd still dither at roundabouts and seek out complex routes through town avoiding right turns.

Perhaps there's something wrong with my spatial awareness, but to be quite frank, I've never truly mastered right and left. Of course, I know my right hand from my left and can raise them swiftly and correctly when asked, but after this the whole thing breaks down. It's never become instinctive. If someone asks me where M&S is, I point and say, "It's down there on your... left." That row of dots indicates the pause in which I translate the clear idea I have in my mind into the correct word. It's as if right and left are new concepts foisted onto me, like decimal currency or metric measurement. Why is this? Giving people directions is almost impossible. "You want to go to that roundabout and turn right," I say. The driver looks at me, hesitates, then ventures, "Um, do you mean that? Because you're actually pointing left...."

The other tricky one is "inside" and "outside" lanes. I always have to think the obvious (ie, "inside" = the lane nearest the middle of the road) then say the opposite. I refer to the correct version as "Colin-speke", because Colin was my BSM instructor. A vicar I know points out, somewhat witheringly, that it's actually Highway Code-speke, and that nobody but me has a problem with it.

These are a few of my least favourite things

Driving

I'm a keen non-driver. Luckily I can dress this up in ecological soundness, but basically I know nothing of the thrill of speed. I appreciate the look of sports cars, but my first thought is, "How long before someone runs a 50p piece along the side?" and the second thought is, "Oh no, I'd have to drive it like a man!" The minute you ventured out of your gates any red-blooded male catching sight of you would think you'd stolen your boyfriend's car and see it as his duty to run you off the road. The only honourable response is to systematically cut them up, race them away from traffic lights with a manly gesture and overtake on the inside on motorways.

I'm just not up to that. My ambition is to adjust the heater without accidentally joining the driver in front in the back seat of his or her car. Or to learn how to adjust your clutch control to the footwear you are sporting on any given day. The first time I ventured out in my Doc Martens was exciting. You can't actually feel the pedals. In fact, it's vaguely reminiscent of attempting a new computer game—what happens if I press this? VOOM! into the gatepost.

Saints of the week

POTAMIAENA AND BASILIDES (3RD C), MARTYRS. FEAST: 28 JUNE.

THIRD SUNDAY AFTER PENTECOST

or

THE SECOND SUNDAY AFTER TRINITY

or

PENTECOST 3
(Trinity 2)
(Ember Day: ie, the Sunday nearest to the
Festival of St Peter [Petertide]. NB Peter the
Apostle may be celebrated alone, without
Paul, on 29 June)
[Proper 5]
(Five for the Symbols at your Door)
(Green)

───────────────

I've come to realize that no matter how modern and liberated we like to think we are, there will always remain some pockets of gender stereotyping. There is nothing like an electrical gadget for ferreting them out. I cannot, for the life of me, fathom things like video machines, but automatic washing machines are a doddle. A vicar I know is the opposite. These blind spots may sound harmless, but they can in fact result in serious marriage-threatening scenarios, eg, accidentally taping the last fifty minutes of the bodice-ripper instead of *Match of the Day*. There's no end to the number of video pitfalls. I've come to dread the words "It's all set up, you just have to press the button." And in the weird world of men there are parallel problems in defining a "whites and light-coloureds" load in such a way as to exclude navy-blue tracksuit bottoms.

Actually, if I'm honest, my incompetence goes way beyond the gender divide. While nobody could reasonably expect me to understand lawnmowers (I might end up having to mow a lawn) I can see that I should be able to work out how to set the cooker clock to three o'clock. I thought I had, until a puzzled guest said, "Have I gone mad or is it that clock going backwards?" I'd set the timer to 15 hours.

*

(That asterisk represents a pause as I break off to tell a vicar I know which sheets to put on the bed.) I'm glad I had the foresight to become a writer. I can always play my ditzy woman novelist card. "Silly me! I've liquidized the tomatoes without the blender lid on, tra la!" Given that words are my medium, strange that I should find Ceefax so baffling. "Suspicious children in house blaze." I was also mystified to read that a man had been "put down"—until someone kindly explained that "One Man" is the name of a horse. The worst was "POOR US to cancel Third World Debt". Well, that's a bit self-pitying, I thought.

These are a few of my least favourite things

Bedtime stories

Boys will be boys. I've just been on bedtime story duty. Tonight's choices were *The Aces: Pilots and Planes of World War I*, followed by *The International Rescue Book of THUNDERBIRDS* with "Fab Cross-sections". Whatever happened to Beatrix Potter? Can I bear the thought that my two sons are growing up understanding Fokker's interrupter gear for controlling forward-facing machine guns, without knowing where the phrase "Tiddly-widdly-widdly, Mrs Tittlemouse" comes from?

Saint of the week

SEXBURGA (7TH C), ABBESS OF ELY. FEAST: 6 JULY.

FOURTH SUNDAY AFTER PENTECOST

or

THIRD SUNDAY AFTER TRINITY

or

PENTECOST 4

(Trinity 3)

(Thomas Becket may be celebrated on
7 July instead of 29 December)

[Proper 6]

(Green)

Every so often, when the wind is in the East, I turn into a real clergy wife and bake Victoria sponges. From time to time I also offer useful tips. As you will have noticed I feel diffident about this, being nothing but a nonconformist in origins, but I've observed that in some Christian circles uselessness is very fashionable. Indeed, you wouldn't presume to address people on any subject in which you actually possess any expertise. "We're here today *not* as experts. We're not claiming to have all the answers. We want to share with you out of our failure and brokenness, our utter cack-handed, blithering, up-cocking incompetence."

Drawing courage from this approach I thought I'd offer a few more household hints. I know that the words "a little hint" can strike terror into the bravest heart. People offering little hints are seldom bearing good news. Bad breath, spinach on teeth, yesterday's knickers emerging from trouser ankle. I hope nobody will feel in any way threatened by my own offerings on hygiene.

I know a lot of people are paranoid about bacteria. I combat this with a choice of soothing mantras: "Never mind—it's a clean floor," or "Never mind—the heat'll kill all the germs." Or (this one to be screamed in a cathartic way), "Oh give it here, for heaven's sake, I'll run it under the tap. There! Satisfied?"

These are a few of my least favourite things

Household gadgets

Household gadgets can be a source of much worry. For instance, the handle on our washing-machine door broke a while back. This is an expensive nuisance, but it does at least provide me with the opportunity to offer you another useful household tip. It is still possible to open your machine if this happens by threading a loop of stout string round the edge of the door and pulling it firmly in the opposite direction to the broken handle, thereby releasing the catch. The catch can be closed by means of a small plastic dagger. In fact, the string and dagger technique is so handy, I don't really know why I bothered having the thing repaired.

Useful gifts

A year or so ago I was lucky enough to receive a book recently titled *Helpful Hints for Housewives* from a Revolutionary Communist I know. A flip through reveals such sections as "How to give your refrigerator the best care" and "wine is fun". I actually knew the last one already, so perhaps I'm not a totally lost cause.

It gave me an idea for my next book, *Helpful Hints for Clergy Spouses*. I venture to hope, in my useless broken way, that much of it will also be not totally without use in lay households. "How to lift Vino Sacro stains out of the brand-new altar cloth that has just been dedicated." "AGMs are fun!" "What to do if the Advent ring catches fire half way through the Eucharistic prayer." "Touching up chipped paintwork in the vicarage with liquid paper." "How to repair a cassock hem with staples or sticky tape." "The church bazaar—always shake silver fish and dead spiders out of jam jars before filling with mincemeat." "The after-confirmation bun fight—never sneeze in front of the bishop when you have just put a handful of peanuts into your mouth."

Vicarage children

I've come to dread any utterance by my sons which begins, "My mum says...." This is never more true than when it is directed at guests. I heard my older son saying it the other day and cried, "Stop! Stop right there!" A lucky premonition. It turned out that he was about to tell them I'd once (apparently, ha ha!) said you could pass guinea-pig droppings off as savoury snacks if you put them in a little bowl. I was in the very act of handing peanuts around as he spoke.

Saint of the week

BOISIL (7TH C), ABBOT OF MELROSE. FEAST: 7 JULY.

FIFTH SUNDAY AFTER PENTECOST

or

THE FOURTH SUNDAY AFTER TRINITY

or

PENTECOST 5

(Trinity 4)

[Proper 6]

(Two, Two the Lily-white Boys, clothed all in)

(Green)

(O)

T he most vicar's-wifey thing I have ever done was to open a garden fête. I said, "I declare this garden fête open." After a short stunned pause (in which everyone registered their good luck that I wasn't going to go on for 45 minutes) I was trampled underfoot in the stampede to the cake stall.

Garden fêtes are bizarre—and bazaars are a worse fate. (This is the kind of feeble joke that provokes my sons to look at me in pained disbelief.) Surely any fund-raising exercise in which people buy a tin of soup for 60p in order to sell it on the grocery stall for 25p needs rethinking. The vicar could raise more by going round shaking a biscuit tin during coffee. But where would be the fun in that? Fun is what it's all about, particularly the hilarious opportunity to put the vicar in the stocks and throw wet sponges at him. (Or her? Do women clergy have to endure this too?)

Now, my idea of a *real* garden party is to throw it on a balmy summer night and have live jazz and champagne. Strangely, everyone in the parish knows this. Last year they even knew the date on which it would occur. Everyone knew, in fact, except a vicar I know. He only discovered during a PCC meeting when others were confidently discussing it. That year we had a Hollywood theme. I made a Peter Pan outfit (or, if we're being pedantic about authentic pronunciation, Peter *Pen*), and an R2D2 costume for my sons. "Wouldn't you rather come as Mowgli from *The Jungle Book*?" I pleaded. "Look, we've got some red underpants already! Or what about the invisible man? You could hide under your bunk all evening." But R2D2 it was. You can do amazing things with a white plastic laundry basket and a large plastic mixing bowl on top.

This year we have a French theme. A vicar I know thought long and hard about coming as Eric Cantona, but decided in the end that the mortification of wearing a Man U kit outweighed the pleasure of kicking his parishioners in the head. He'll be coming instead as John Calvin, the popular choice.

There are a couple of things which I will always associate with the morning after a vicarage garden party. One is thriftily washing and drying all those plastic glasses to re-use next year. The other is seeing the grass scattered with feathers from a dozen boas, as though several exotic birds had been shot on the lawn. And best of all, the full wine rack. The good thing about Evangelicals is that they *always* bring more booze than they consume.

These are a few of my least favourite things

Gardening

Garden parties mean a lot of preparation. Mowing lawns, turning a flame-thrower on the weeds on the patio, chucking rotting carpets over the fence into the neighbours' yard. But I'm beginning to wonder if I'm just too garden-proud. After all, people don't come to the vicarage garden party to admire my herbaceous borders. Indeed, if last year was anything to go by, after a glass of rum punch they won't even find the borders, apart from in a very sudden and intimate way, by falling face down into them. A stiff bevvy at the door cuts out hours of tedious weeding, I always find.

*"...and I was thinking of a water feature here—big and splashy to
sober the parishioners up before they drive home."*

Handy hints from the vicar's wife

Rum punch recipe

Carton of orange juice, bottle of Cava, half a bottle of rum, big bottle of ginger beer, loads of ice. Mix in large bucket or portable font.

Saint of the week

PECHTELM (8TH C), NORTHUMBRIAN MISSIONARY. FEAST: 16 JULY.

SIXTH SUNDAY AFTER PENTECOST

or

FIFTH SUNDAY AFTER TRINITY

or

PENTECOST 6
(Trinity 5)
(Where the reference is made to a collocational restriction, the collocational word is either ignored or represented by the appropriate equivalent word in parenthesis.)
[Proper 7]
(Green)

═══════════════

Up and down the land parents are bracing themselves for six weeks of children under their feet and having to find something for them to do. That "something" has, by definition, to be anything other than the thing that parents suggest. Tidying the bedroom doesn't seem to count as an intelligent option for the bored school child. What they want to do is go into town and buy Pokemon booster packs. Or rather, have Pokemon booster packs bought for them.

I'm beginning to think that these last few days of the school year bring with them a marked deterioration in behaviour. Children who are normally biddable seem to be turning into ratbags. I've decided that mine are getting in a little practice for when they are teenagers. Over last weekend I was privileged to witness sneak previews of the storms ahead. Acres of rant can be reduced to a single line: "Why do you always make me do what I don't want to do?" (Is there a Herod's Day, patron of small boys, by the way?)

After a little bit of questioning I uncovered a strange but firmly-held belief that grown-ups get to do exactly what they want the whole time. Well, as you can imagine, I spent some time setting the record straight, but it did take me right back to my childhood when I shared the same belief. Around this time of year we used to sing a rude song which began "One more day in school". I can still remember the line "We do all the rotten work, teachers get the money!" and how that captured *perfectly* the gross unfairness of the situation we found ourselves in.

I suppose that from a child's point of view they spend most of their time being forced to go to school against their will. Education feels like a curse not a blessing. Occasionally I remind my sons that 150 years ago children their age were working down the mines or up the chimneys, to which they predictably reply they'd rather do that than go to school.

These are a few of my least favourite things

The mum's race

One of the great things about inner-city schools is that they often don't have their own sports field. This is totally selfish of me, I admit. Poor old children, confined to hard tarmac playgrounds! But it does mean, in the case of my sons' school, that sports' day only comes round when your children are in Year 2.

When my older son was that age I went, like a good mother, to his sports' day. A vicar I know had to leave before the dads' race, SADLY; which left me as the sole parental figure able to do the honourable thing and enter the mums' race. Now what is the etiquette here? Obviously spiked running shoes would look like you were taking it all too seriously, but what about warming up? Is it better to risk injury by not stretching and bending first; or to risk looking a prat by

"Darling, I'm sorry. I was so looking forward to the Mummys' race."

doing forty star-jumps and still coming last? My son began by begging me to enter, but when I agreed and kicked off my silly shoes and hitched up my dress he changed his tune. "It's all right, Mum, you don't have to." Hah! Think I'll disgrace you, eh? Well, I came second, ta da! The challenge since then has been to walk upstairs without a 45-minute break half way. But the worst bit of the whole ordeal was seeing all the dads and male teachers lined up at the finishing tape, admiring the *Baywatch* effect under cover of cheering us on.

Saints of the week

THE SEVEN SLEEPERS OF EPHESUS. SIXTH-CENTURY LEGEND HAS IT THAT THEY TOOK REFUGE IN A CAVE TO ESCAPE PERSECUTION. GOD PUT THEM TO SLEEP AND THEY WOKE TWO CENTURIES LATER TO FIND THEIR CITY CONVERTED TO CHRISTIANITY. PATRON OF ALL PARENTS WHO WISH GOD WOULD PUT THEM TO SLEEP SO THAT THEY COULD WAKE SIX WEEKS LATER AND FIND THE CHILDREN HAVE GONE BACK TO SCHOOL. FEAST: 27 JULY.

SEVENTH SUNDAY AFTER PENTECOST

or

THE SIXTH SUNDAY AFTER TRINITY

or

PENTECOST 7

(The Transfiguration of our Lord, 6 August,
unless it is observed on the last Sunday
after Epiphany)

(Trinity 6)

[Proper 8]

(Sage green)

═══════════════

What to do, what to do? You've made salt-dough donkey droppings (sorry, vases), you've been to the library, you've played in the park. At some point you will be so far lost to reason that suddenly a shopping trip with school-age children strikes you as a good way of spending an afternoon. I have always believed that shopping centres offer us a glimpse of hell. Why more people don't run stark raving mad down the malls is beyond me. I can remember feeling peculiar in the Arndale centre in Luton which I used to visit as a young teenager.

Of course, shopping centres in the seventies were small fry compared with today's leviathans. If you came over funny back then you could pop up for air pretty easily, but nowadays there remains the horrible possibility that you may drop in to a mall one November lunchtime for a spot of Christmas shopping and still be wandering about looking for an exit 40 years later. That's only one hellish aspect. The other is the relentlessness of it all, the questing after the infinitely receding mirage of material satisfaction. A thousand shops of clothes beyond the stretch of your budget and a million mirrors to remind you how fat, frumpy and generally unworthy you are of being in this Aladdin's cave of consumer bliss.

Perhaps, like me, you read a while ago about a tacit acknowledgement of how dangerous these places are. There are plans afoot to install defibrillators in shopping precincts so that heart-attack victims can be jump-started in the comfort of House of Fraser without having to wait till the ambulance arrives. Staff will be trained to use them and lives will undoubtedly be saved. The devices will be dotted around, I imagine, like fire extinguishers. I hope that, unlike fire extinguishers, they will be kept under lock and key. Letting off gallons of foam for a lark is one thing, but randomly zapping your fellow shoppers is another.

These are a few of my least favourite things

IKEA

I had a nightmare the other night. I'd murdered someone and been convicted and sent to gaol where I was given the most terrible disastrous perm. This was far more harrowing than the fact that I'd killed someone. The thought of not seeing my sons cost me a pang, but that was nothing compared to the horror of seeing my reflection in the prison salon mirror.

I'm sure the dream was fuelled by guilt, layer upon layer of it. It's true. I went to IKEA last Saturday. After all I've said in my time about frivolous journeys and that great Swedish shrine to resource-gobbling consumerism! And worse—in my quest for some cardboard storage boxes called Peng I lost my children. Somewhere between plants and glassware I carelessly glanced away and they were warped into a parallel dimension, which I gather happens all the time at IKEA. If the truth be told it was quite a while before I actually noticed. I was assuming they were around somewhere, possibly in the china section experimenting to find out why the mugs were called "Bang".

"When I said she needed mouth to mouth I didn't mean to send for Ms. Roberts from cosmetics to give her a full facial... Hello? emergency services?"

Eventually it dawned on me that they'd vanished and I was left with a dilemma. Should I press on and assume I'd find them at the end? Or would they try to retrace their steps?

In the end I tried both. Retracing your steps in IKEA on a Saturday afternoon has long and, I think, unfairly been overlooked as an Olympic sport. Eventually the tannoy went "Bing-bong! Would Catherine Fox make her way to the information desk and claim her Worst Mother of the Day award." The trick here is not to identify yourself to onlookers by starting, looking guilt-stricken and plunging off in what you hope will be the right direction. People will stare and point if you do, and murmur that you don't deserve to have children. Next time you'll have to go shopping in disguise. Maybe a perm would be a good idea after all.

Saint of the week

SIDWELL (9TH C?), VIRGIN MARTYR.
HER STEPMOTHER INCITED REAPERS TO SCYTHE HER HEAD OFF.
FEAST: 31 JULY.

"Old Ma Sidwell was right—it was an 'orrible perm."

EIGHTH SUNDAY AFTER PENTECOST

or

THE SEVENTH SUNDAY AFTER TRINITY

or

PENTECOST 8
(Trinity 7)
(The Blessed Virgin Mary may be celebrated on 8 September instead of 15 August)
[Proper 9]
(Emerald green)

═══════════════

So you've done IKEA, you've done the shopping mall. There's only one thing left—the local garden centre. It's important to do this on The Sabbath, of course. That's where everyone else goes to worship. Until I went last week I hadn't realized the sheer scale of fervent garden devotion that goes on in this country. The statue section alone left me stunned. There are three categories: animals, faintly pornographic female nudes and St Francis. He had his eyes modestly fixed upon the bird in his hand, rather than on all the scantily clad ones in the bushes round about. There was a mystifying sign hanging from the ceiling which read "Self-contained garden ornaments". Perhaps it referred to him.

Gardens are a source of continuing irritation to the clergy. Along with lying in bed reading the papers, they offer the most serious competition to church attendance. People are quick to justify themselves: "Ah well, you don't have to go to a church, do you?

'You're nearer to God in a garden than anywhere else on earth', eh vicar?" They occasionally add, "As the Good Book says." The Good Book in question presumably being the complete poems of Dorothy Gurney. Unfortunately I don't have the text in front of me. I've just consulted my volume of *Poems with Power to Strengthen the Soul* compiled by James Mudge—but in vain. *The Dictionary of Quotations* reveals that people usually get it wrong. "One is nearer God's heart in a garden/Than anywhere else on earth" is how it should go.

This could be a serious theological point, referring back to God's original creation of the Garden of Eden. When we toil and create something beautiful in our own gardens, are we indeed close to the heart of the creator? This will depend on how much you like gardening, of course. I'm in the happy position of being able to enjoy the fruits of other people's labours. All I have to do is mow the lawn occasionally. Or rather, mention occasionally to a vicar I know that it needs mowing. Lots of lovely hardy perennials and a postmodern garden shed. It was deconstructed by next door's tree in a storm.

It's worth remembering, though, that God's purposes don't end with Eden, but with the New Jerusalem; not with the happy couple relaxing in the privacy of their lovely garden, but in the people of God living in community. It might be truer to say, "One is nearer God's heart in the city than anywhere else on earth."

Handy hints from the vicar's wife

How to clear the patio

The trouble with garden centres is that you come away glumly dissatisfied with the state of your own garden. I know I'll never have one of those glorious plots that can be opened to the admiring public. All we could realistically offer would be a feel-good factor to other struggling horticulturalists. "At least we haven't got a muddy crater filled with Action Man limbs where the pond used to be," people would think. Then there's the assault course aspect: out through the French windows and flat on your face on the algae-slimed patio. A vicar I know has declared war on this slime. "It's amazing what you can do with a bucket of bleach and a fish slice," he says. This is probably a wise precaution if we intend to have people round for a barbeque this summer. He doesn't want to be completely tied up over the following six months visiting parishioners with broken hips. On the other hand, we might make a feature of it. We could hose the area down and advertise it as summer skating at the vicarage.

Saint of the week

JAMBERT (8TH C), ARCHBISHOP OF CANTERBURY. FEAST: 12 AUGUST.

NINTH SUNDAY AFTER PENTECOST

or

THE EIGHTH SUNDAY AFTER TRINITY

or

PENTECOST 9
Fat and Useless Sunday
(Trinity 8)
[Improper 10]
(British racing green)

For many of us these are the last few desperate days of trying to get in shape before the annual poolside humiliation. A vicar I know has been doing press-ups and sit-ups and going for long punishing runs which leave him unable to get up out of his chair and answer the phone. I had to fob a parishioner off shortly after he staggered back in this afternoon by promising he'd ring them back. It was either that or five minutes of pastoral heavy breathing. All this in pursuit of a six-pack.

It was a while before I saw the meaning of this image. I kept visualizing the cans sideways on, which looks surprisingly like rolls of fat if you think about it. It means a six-pack views from above, of course, and that's a six-pack of lager by the way, not mini cereal packets or economy kitchen roll. A curate I know maintains that his six-pack is kept safely in the cool bag under a layer of insulation. But hey, at least it's not still down the off-licence. Other men seem to have gone a bit overboard on the alcoholic imagery and sport an entire keg of ale around their middles.

These are a few of my least favourite things

Cheap flights on the Internet

The other seasonal form of work-out is a mental one. It's called "Finding a cheap flight on the Internet". There are any number of outfits offering astoundingly cheap flights. The only two snags you invariably hit are the fact that they are going from the wrong destination on the wrong day. This is a matter of honour and principle with the agencies concerned. I've been listening in as a vicar I know plays cat and mouse with the unfortunate person at the other end of the phone. The conversation goes:

Vicar: "I'm interested in the flight to Cyprus advertised at £69."

Agent: "When do you wish to travel?"

Vicar: "I don't mind. Tell me about that flight."

Agent: "Where are you travelling from?"

Vicar: "I don't mind. Tell me about the flight advertised at £69."

Agent: (after a short pause) "Bear with me while I consult my supervisor.... "

A cynic might almost conclude that there is no flight to Cyprus at £69, or that they are waiting for you to say you want to fly from Birmingham so that they can reply, "Oh, I'm terribly sorry, that flight is a special offer from Glasgow." What they'd say if you responded with "OK I'll go from Glasgow then" I don't know. Probably "Oops! I've just sold the last one." I sometimes wonder if, while they put you on hold to consult their supervisor, the music playing is "Oh bury me not on the lone prairie" or "Goodbye, old Paint".

Needless to say, the children were left completely out of the holiday destination discussion. What on earth is the point of asking them where they want to go when you know full well that you're only going to say, "Well, you can't"? You can't go to Disneyland, Paris and you can't go to Japan to buy Pokemon silver or gold version. I suppose you could ask them, say no, and call it a process of consultation. After all, we are Anglicans.

Saint of the week

PHILIBERT (7TH C), ABBOT AND FOUNDER OF JUMIEGES. FEAST: 20 AUGUST.

TENTH SUNDAY AFTER PENTECOST

or

THE NINTH SUNDAY AFTER TRINITY

or

PENTECOST 10
(Trinity 9)
[Proper 11]
(Lincoln green)

═══════════════════

Actually, I'm having a concentrated attempt not to be a ratbag this holiday. I had a horrible dream last night that my younger son died. This keeps springing back into my mind as I catch myself snarling in frustration at him for some trivial reason. At least he's there to snarl at, I remind myself. In fact, he's just come in now to ask when we're going to write "Johnny Expert goes to the Moon", our first collaborative fiction venture. He dictates and I type. I've no idea what will emerge, as quite frankly, the child has a bizarre take on the world. He told me the other day that he wanted a guinea pig for his birthday. "But what shall I call it?" he worried. "You can call it whatever you like," I reassured. After a moment's thought he said, "I'm going to call it the F-word." This notion was enthusiastically taken up by my older son, who immediately improvised a scene called "Calling the lost guinea pig in the garden". I don't think the younger one knows what the "F" stands for. "Fat", probably, as that's the thing he knows he's not allowed to call me.

If my bad dream came true my world would fill up with self-recrimination. Why did I sit writing books not Johnny Expert? Why didn't I buy him a dozen guinea pigs to exhaust his list of obscenities? It's only after tragedy has struck that we wish we'd spent our time differently. We know that. But given that we know it, why can't we translate that knowledge into action? Why are we still locked in permanent exasperation with the ones we could never do without? I think it's because we are hemmed in on every side by time, by our own finiteness. It's only just beginning to dawn on me that this is what it means to be a sinner. Not the sinful acts we commit so much as being trapped in our lives like a bluebottle in a jam jar. The glass walls are death and there's nothing we can do about it.

Handy hints from the vicar's wife

Going on holiday

There are all sorts of possibilities for the vicarage family when it comes to summer holidays. The only thing that really never worked is "just staying quietly at home". You would have to stay quietly at home behind razor wire with a bazooka trained on the gate if you really want parishioners to understand that you're on holiday.

One option is The Locum, where you go and stay for free in some other vicarage in a glamorous location in exchange for Sunday duties. Trotting out your sermon on St Swythun in exchange for lounging about on a tropical beach—not bad, eh? We've never done this. We usually go for the option called Sponging off Wealthier Friends. Most clergy know of people with holiday homes that they let at a reasonable rate to impoverished parsons. Failing all else you can rent some amazing-sounding luxury accommodation you see advertised in the church press which will turn out to be damp, clapped-out and have curtains dating from the 1970s that nobody liked even back then. But we won't complain, no no, not even if we give up and go home half way through the holiday. This is one of the joys and privileges of being a Christian. We allow our brothers and sisters in Christ to rip us off.

Saint of the week

BREGWINE (8TH C), ARCHBISHOP OF CANTERBURY. FEAST: 26 AUGUST.

ELEVENTH SUNDAY AFTER PENTECOST

or

THE TENTH SUNDAY AFTER TRINITY

or

PENTECOST 11

(Trinity 10)

(If a 21-pin SCART/PERITEL lead has been used,
this procedure may be omitted)
[Proper 12]
(Chartreuse or Eau de Nil)

═══════════

*W*ell, that's the summer holiday nearly survived. We've been enjoying all those traditional end-of-vacation games like hunt the PE bag, trying to buy a lunchbox without Barbie or Teletubbies on it and seeing if we can sit in Clarke's shoe shop for 45 minutes without loss of life. And today we have naming of uniform parts.

Where do all the grey school socks go? Or rather, where do half of them go? It's easy to dismiss them as dull, but grey school socks are as rich and varied a species as you could encounter anywhere in the natural world. So many sub-species and subtle varieties! They are endlessly evolving, sprouting holes and little ladders, shedding their elastic, fading and shrinking, never the same for two weeks together. A novice might assume that, arriving in pairs, they mate for life. Not a bit of it. Theirs is a life of wanton coupling, long with short, ribbed with plain ("Huh! Brilliant pair of socks, Mum." "It's those or nothing! You find a pair if you're that fussy!") In fact, the one thing that's sadly evident in socks' social behaviour is that they renounce monogamy at the earliest opportunity.

I've come to the conclusion that although they may mate, they disappear somewhere else to hatch their offspring. This is the obvious explanation for the fact that you only ever lose one sock, not a pair. It is presumably the female that migrates to the ancient sock birthing grounds never to be seen again. I've also noted the presence of one dominant Alpha male grey

"I think we should move the chest of drawers away from the radiator."

sock in the sock box in the laundry room, a predator from the adult sock drawer. No matter how often he is evicted, he reappears.

Once, when tidying my sons' bedroom for the first time in months, I disturbed several pairs of hibernating grey socks. I was also thrilled to discover that they live, apparently, on a diet of cheesy wotsits. I found a great many fossilized remains of this snack distributed throughout the school socks' natural habitat. Socks are shy and retiring creatures, preferring the backs of bookcases and the darkest corners of plastic toy crates to the expanse of open carpet that from time to time opens up when a frustrated adult kicks a path clear to the window.

Handy hints from the vicar's wife

When it comes to labelling uniforms, my advice is don't faff about with woven tapes. I noticed a while back that red ballpoint pen never washes out of clothes, so why not just write your child's name on the garment label? Slightly tricky if you buy cheapo seconds clothes with the label cut out by the manufacturer, admittedly.

Great church traditions

Rewriting hymns

Every so often a vicar I know expresses his impatience with the wording of various hymns and songs. I've heard him sit with a Baptist minister I know and work on corrections to theologically suspect lines: "Jesus loves me, this I know/For the Bible (and the inner witness of the Holy Spirit) tells me so," was one of their suggestions. "The existence of God, Creation's voice implies it," was another. "Jesus, we enthrone you" always strikes me as a bit impertinent, as does "Holy Spirit we welcome you". I'd be a bit taken aback if I was greeted on my own doorstep with the words "Welcome to St Paul's vicarage!" But it's the lovey-dovey songs that are most likely to bring out the curmudgeonly streak in this vicar I know. He can't be doing with any language about "falling more deeply in love" with Jesus. Completely inappropriate, he finds it. But they're drawing on the imagery of the Song of Songs, I point out in my annoying way. They aren't, of course. The Song of Songs is about physical, sexual love, not modern Western romance. These songs draw on pop culture where Jesus is reduced to the role of cosmic boyfriend.

Saints of the week

FELIX AND ADAUCTUS (4TH C), MARTYRS. FEAST: 30 AUGUST.

TWELFTH SUNDAY AFTER PENTECOST

or

THE ELEVENTH SUNDAY AFTER TRINITY

or

PENTECOST 12
(Trinity 11)
[Proper 13]
(Pea or apple green)

I remember reading in *The Independent* once about a piece of research which showed that "the average person in Britain spends a year of their life looking for lost items". Personally, I would be interested to see a breakdown of the figures, as I suspect that hidden in this statistic is the fact that mothers spend twenty years of their lives hunting for their children's lost things, with PE kit coming out top of the list. The house is always awash with white T-shirts and navy-blue shorts all through the holidays. You cannot walk through a room without tripping over black elasticated pumps *except* on the day when PE starts again and all you can find is the swimming kit that has been perversely elusive for the last half term.

According to the article, the top four lost items are money, keys, TV remote and knickers. I don't see the problem with knickers, mind you. I always know where they are—in the laundry basket waiting to be washed. Here in the vicarage we don't lose money so much as accidentally spend it.

Mislaid keys and TV remote sound familiar. The usual suspect is an old sofa which is so shot to pieces that it could eat a small child,

"Mum, Rodney's Dad says can Rodney come round
and sit on our sofa for a while!"

let alone an electronic gadget. You leave your offspring watching *Aladdin* and come back later to see just a leg protruding. Like seeing a chunky draylon anaconda swallowing a deer.

The survey also asked people what they would most like to lose. Weight, predictably, came out top, followed by wrinkles/spots. One of the saddest revelations was the fact that half of those questioned "were keen to lose boring friends". I can sympathize with temporarily mislaying them, but to lose them altogether is a loss indeed. An alarming one in twelve wanted to lose their current partner. It strikes me that the people conducting the survey must have forgotten to ask one thing—would you like to lose your guilty conscience, your sense of failure? Would you like to lose all those things which still have the power to make you break out in a cold sweat at 4 am as you lie unable to sleep? Would you, in short, like to feel forgiven? I'd rank that even higher than losing my moustache.

Great church traditions

Going computerized

In the olden days of scribes and vellum, nobody could have foreseen the golden age of typewriters and church duplicators. How dizzying to be living in an era when those laudable innovations are a thing of the past.

A vicar I know has just bought a new computer. It's one of those machines that does everything; or would, if we knew what we were about, and will, when the various non-working components are replaced. It scans, it photographs, it faxes, it plays games, it's voice activated, it does the housework ("Mum, can I play on the new computer?" "When you've tidied your bedroom.") My sons use it to play Tomb Raider 3 and have found a way of making Lara Croft explode. She always looks just on the brink of a twin explosion anyway.

My favourite is the voice recognition dictation. It does strange things to hymns, as a vicar I know discovered when dictating an order of service:

And can it bleed when flat hat IRA should gain
An interest in the Saviour's blood
Died he for me who caused his play
For me, who him to death of her sued?
Amazing Love, how can eight p
The vat that vile, my God, should keep up at 400.

The computer went on to "Tis Mr Roux all" and "to sour the depths of love divine Kitty". For some reason it has an urge to include as many proper nouns as possible, as in "Clive, King of Heaven" from "Be thou my vision":

Hiking of heaven when battle is damned
Grant heaven's jury's tummy O'Brien taverns Sams
Christ of my own heart whatever befalls Colin
Still be my vision O ruler of all.

Saint of the week

DISIBOD (7TH C), IRISH BISHOP. FEAST: 8 SEPTEMBER.

THIRTEENTH SUNDAY AFTER PENTECOST

or

THE TWELFTH SUNDAY AFTER TRINITY

or

PENTECOST 13
(Trinity 12)
[Proper 14]
(Bottle green)

Every so often I am struck afresh by the strangeness of the world I inhabit. Take the concept of licensing, for instance. This is another of those churchy words that you don't think about unless someone from outside asks you what it means. Before we moved to Walsall I remember talking about the licensing of a vicar I know, and an atheist friend of mine asked if he would get a licence to put up on the wall, like in a bar. "Licensed to serve alcoholic communion beverages", perhaps?

For me the word always conjures up James Bond. Cleric 007— licensed to preach. "The name's Bond. Reverend James Bond. I take my tea sugared but not stirred." I can picture him in a white DJ over a black clerical shirt doing battle with some crazed megalomaniac bishop who is bent on taking over the world and breeding a new master race of superpriests. "Ah, Mr Bond. A pleasure to meet you. I'm sorry our acquaintance will be of short duration. I am about to press this button which will set in motion your lengthy and complicated execution, while I inexplicably go away to chair a diocesan peace and justice sub-committee without ensuring you are actually dead."

"Do what you like with me, but let the deacon go. She knows nothing. She trained at Westcott."

But perhaps it's more like a driving licence. The holder could be done for preaching without due care and attention, for undue hesitancy, preaching while under the influence of alcohol, for using incorrect hand signals, exceeding the speed limit, and for failing to stop. I've heard some evangelistic sermons which do the homiletic equivalent of mounting the kerb and mowing down innocent pedestrians. Ban them.

Handy hints from the vicar's wife

How to be an image consultant

A big danger for vicars is that of getting stuck in a fashion time warp. Our role as clergy spouses is to prevent this. We have to utter those unpalatable truths like "Why not buy the next size up, then you won't have to suck in during deanery synod." Another thing we can do is buy them clothes.

A while ago I went to a jeans shop and started looking for a pair of black jeans for a vicar I know. I was wondering out loud what size to buy to a roofer's wife I know who had gone with me. The owner of the shop overheard and asked, "Was the gentleman in the shop about a week ago buying a pair of blue jeans?" I said, "Yes," and having established that we were talking about the same gentleman, the shopkeeper said, "I think you'll find the gentleman didn't buy 501s. The gentleman bought 522s because the gentleman had thick-set legs."

"Do you mean muscular thighs?" I demanded in my best Lady Bracknell voice. As far as the shopkeeper remembered, the gentleman had bought 32-long ("Because the gentleman had a long leg,") 522s. I must say, I was won over by this impressive recall of customer details and followed his advice. I gave the jeans to a vicar I know and said, "Here, try these on yer thick-set legs, my boy." It turned out that Dennis, for that was the shopkeeper's name, was right. They fitted perfectly. A tall order, you might think, for a vicar with thick-set legs, one of them long. Dennis also had a piece of advice which I gladly pass on to all you black jeans owners—wash and iron them inside out and you'll double their life. Apart from the ludicrous bit about ironing, the suggestion is sound.

Saint of the week

ADAM OF CAITHNESS (13TH C), MARTYRED FOR GRINDING
THE FACE OF THE POOR BY ENFORCING DRACONIAN TYTHES ON
INNOCENT LAW-ABIDING PEASANTS (IE, MARTYR IN THE TRADITION OF
CHARLES, KING AND "MARTYR", PAH!). FEAST: 15 SEPTEMBER.

FOURTEENTH SUNDAY AFTER PENTECOST

or

THE THIRTEENTH SUNDAY AFTER TRINITY

or

PENTECOST 14
(Trinity 13)
[Proper 15]
(Grass or moss green)

'***I***'ve been experiencing a certain light-heartedness over the last week. There has been a new spring in my step that has nothing to do with my Nike air-wear trainers, or whatever they're called. I bought them a few weeks back because I had a sudden grim image of myself in the future crippled with arthritic knees and thinking, "If only I'd bought myself proper trainers back in my late thirties." Have you ever tried to buy trainers, by the way? In the olden days you went to a shop and asked for plimsolls. They said, "Black or white?" and that, apart from size, was that.

As it was, I ventured into a sports shop with the demeanour of a man in a lingerie department hoping to get something for his girlfriend without actually knowing her size or taste. Trust me, I know that look. I've worked in lingerie departments. I was full of helpful tips like, "Is she shortsighted, sir? In which case, don't buy her anything with a snap-fastening crotch, because if, for reasons of vanity, she leaves her glasses at home, she'll never be able to do herself up in the restaurant loo."

My first problem in the sports shop was the fact that the radio was so loud I ended up practically semaphoring to the assistant what I wanted. "R-U-N-N-I-N-G S-H-O-E-S C-H-E-A-P." My advice is that you buy a size bigger than you think you need because sports socks are thick and your feet swell up when you run. The result is that my Nikes look like smallish sailing vessels. Hovercrafts, perhaps, given the air-cushioned soles.

But, as I said, that's not why I had a spring in my step. The lightness was to do with having done my tax. No longer am I menaced by the bowler-hatted berk in the adverts saying smugly, "Now's the time...."

"Aw, come on Guv. Charity giving's tax deductible."

I think my feelings about Inland Revenue are similar to many people's attitude to God— months of denial punctured by crises of bleating paranoia. A friend of mine once told me about the moment when her accountant said to her, "I need you to sign here to say I can act as your representative to Inland Revenue." She said she almost kissed him. At last, a mediator to stand between her and the taxman! I think the potential for sermon illustrations here is obvious enough.

Handy hints from the vicar's wife

How to buy new clothes without annoying your spouse

What is it about clothes shopping that causes otherwise reasonable women to revert to crude stereotypes of female deviousness? We all know that old ploy of hiding a new dress in the wardrobe for a month, then saying, "This? No, I've had it ages." If you want to descend one rung lower on the ladder of female deviousness you can turn this into an accusation of male insensitivity. "Huh! Shows how much notice *you* take of what I look like!"

Most men are fine about clothes buying if they are warned in advance. But why is it so difficult to do this? It's because we view clothes as a wearable form of chocolate, something you indulge in guiltily when you're feeling low, or to celebrate feeling high, or because you happen to be walking past the shop. Men, on the other hand, seem to regard clothes as staple food. If they're hungry, they eat something. If their knees start to show through their trousers, they buy a new pair. I can never banish the lurking belief that my expenditure is frivolous and self indulgent. This is why I say (airily), "Oh, I bought some new trousers, by the way." Then add, "But they only cost three pounds!"

Typo of the week

"AS WE GRAZE ON YOUR KINGLY BRIGHTNESS."

Saint of the week

FIRMIN (4TH C), BISHOP AND MARTYR. FEAST: 25 SEPTEMBER.

FIFTEENTH SUNDAY AFTER PENTECOST

or

THE FOURTEENTH SUNDAY AFTER TRINITY

or

PENTECOST 15
(Trinity 14)
(Ember Day, ie Sunday nearest to
St Michael and All Angels [Michaelmas])
[Proper 16]
(Lime green)

═══════════════

Every so often a strange blip occurs in the far-off world of the catwalk which accidentally renders clergy fashionable. Take the tank top, for instance. Most of us threw ours out in 1978, but a great many vicars quietly persisted in wearing them, under the description "sleeveless pullover", and lo and behold, the big wheel turns and they are a fashion item once more. I imagine that a small ripple of satisfaction passed through vicarages up and down the land when the news broke a while back that "grey is the new black". I was flipping the pages of a vestments catalogue the other day and saw a garment which managed to be both grey *and* a tank top, so double points there for the Vanpoulles "Guernsey slip-over".

These brochures repay careful study. They open up a whole new world to low-church persons like me. I've been trying to imagine who might wear a "sleeveless casual cassock". Is it something high churchmen slip into when they want to be more comfortable?

Another key fashion item at the moment is the knee-length knife-pleated skirt. The knife-pleat theme translates quite happily into the vestment world. Those of you with five pleats in your cassock are laughing. Let's add those different elements together and see what we've got. A knee-length grey sleeveless knife-pleated cassock. Sounds like a gym-slip to me.

Another key feature at the moment is fringing and tassels. I think we Evangelicals can forget those. They sound a bit car-tholic to me. Birettas and that stuff. (Although most decent cassocks have a tiny fringe around the hem. I used to think that was because they'd all frayed, but I now know it's sewn there deliberately. I'm not sure why. To dust the chancel floor, perhaps, and save on vergers' fees?) Likewise we can dismiss the "backless tops and dresses"—no, wait! Do stocks count? They're backless clerical shirts, aren't they? All in all, the latest fashion trends are good news for the church. I think that even bishops need not entirely despair. As far as I can see all kinds of patterned, highly decorative and embroidered garments are in. The poncho is making a big come-back, and what's a cope, really, if it's not a floor-length poncho?

Great church traditions

Buying a new cassock

One of the highlights of my life in recent years was a trip to a clerical outfitters. I find the whole vestments thing quite thrilling—starved in my formative years, you see, except for the odd Geneva preaching gown.

I was accompanying a vicar I know who needed a new cassock. Up till then he had worn one inherited from his father, but after a good 35 years of service it was beginning to show signs of wear. In my innocence I thought buying a cassock was a bit like buying rubber gloves, only without the exciting colour range. I soon discovered it's more like buying jeans—so complex that you almost dissolve in tears of despair. You have to decide between single and double breasted; one, three or five back pleats; whether you want wool or polyester, and what weight and type of weave. Then you enter a realm of detail so elevated (concerning soutanes and the like) that I've decided to simplify things for the reader by calling it poncy or non-poncy.

Next comes the measuring. One assistant takes measurements, then calls them out to another who writes them down. Chest, back, shoulder, waist, arm—you name it. "What about front?" called the second assistant. "We don't need it," said the first. "The gentleman doesn't have a pot."

Saints of the week

COSMAS AND DAMIAN (DATE UNKNOWN), TWINS.
AMONG THEIR REMARKABLE ACTS WAS THE SUCCESSFUL GRAFTING
OF A WHITE LEG ONTO A BLACK MAN SUFFERING FROM CANCER.
PATRONS OF DOCTORS AND MALE HAIRDRESSERS.
FEAST: 26 SEPTEMBER.

Handy hint from the vicar's wife

Men—forget your local Greek barber. Why not celebrate St Cosmas and St Damian's Day by going to a proper hair salon and having a decent haircut?

SIXTEENTH SUNDAY AFTER PENTECOST

or

THE FIFTEENTH SUNDAY AFTER TRINITY

or

PENTECOST 16
(Trinity 15)
(Dedication Festival—The First sunday in
October or The Last Sunday after Trinity,
if date unknown)
[Proper 17]
(Turquoise or aquamarine)

I often say that I don't have a Call to the Inner City. I have merely married one. I have also married an obsession with football and, in particular, with Newcastle United. I don't really mind that football's coming home. I just wish it wouldn't reel in drunk and knock the ornaments over. When there is an important match on, a vicar I know frequently discovers that there really is quite a bit of work he could more sensibly do at home that evening.

If the Premier League is one end of the footballing spectrum, then inter-church matches are the other. Last summer our church was challenged by another local church. We were encouraged by the rumour that they had lost their previous match 19–1, but that might have been deliberate disinformation. I was surprised at how much I enjoyed it. I was only spectating, of course. Half our team didn't have proper football boots and the clatter of studded feet across the school playground as the opposition arrived was faintly ominous.

However, I'm proud to say that we won 3–1. We supporters have to take some of the credit. We provided lots of very loud, ill-informed encouragement: "Yes! Yes! Kick it! Which way are we playing?" "Shouldn't we chant something?" someone asked. The only thing we could think of was the nunc dimittis. Our "'ere we go, 'ere we go, 'ere we go" had to be altered to "there it went" as the ball was kicked over the fence into the canal. Since then I've been mugging up on chanting etiquette for our next fixture. Apparently the correct form for taunting the other side's goalie is either "Dodgy keepah!" or "You're s*** A-A-A!" I look forward to practising *that* with the churchwardens' wives during coffee after the service.

Football explodes the myth that the average British male feels silly singing. If only we could harness all this raw enthusiasm and get it into church. Mind you, I expect most clergy could do without roars of "Dodgy preachah!" during the sermon.

If the good Lord had intended us to play football he would have given us studs on our feet

My sporting trivia is pretty impressive for one not remotely interested in ball games. I gain it by osmosis from the atmosphere. When I say trivia I mean real trivia, of course. My mind operates a filter system which is the reverse of sieving. It retains tiny insignificant things (eg. name of player's hair stylist), but is incapable of holding on to the big stuff—like the off-side rule. If I ever watch a match I need little refresher courses throughout the game: "So who's playing again?" "Who do we want to win?"

Surprisingly enough, I bear football no ill will. It first impinged on my life when I was a Girls' Brigader. Our national Albert Hall Rally was always on cup final day. I remind myself of this if I'm ever put out by my husband's sporting obsessions. At least I'll never again have to get into an underground train packed with thousands of baying football fans *while wearing a GB uniform*.

These are a few of my least favourite things

The World Cup

There's nothing like the World Cup for creating football widows. I have a few suggestions to make. If you're feeling left out, why not use the time profitably to catch up on those irksome household tasks—like hoovering the sitting room, strimming or mowing noisily outside the window, getting out the electric drill and putting up a few shelves, or hiring a small JCB and tearing up the patio. Remember to call brightly, "Sorry! Won't be long, darling!" over the racket.

If this sounds a bit un-restful, then what about shopping as a good way of filling those tedious hours? "I'm leaving the children with you while I just pop out to IKEA," you call when kick-off is imminent. "Don't worry—I've got the Access card."

Saint of the week

Iwi (7th C), Northumbrian monk and deacon. Feast: 8 October.

SEVENTEENTH SUNDAY AFTER PENTECOST

or

THE SIXTEENTH SUNDAY AFTER TRINITY

or

PENTECOST 17

(Trinity 16)

[Proper 18]

(Slime green)

I think it's time to broach that most difficult of subjects: sex and the clergy. If you look in the press there are two basic kinds of story. 1) Clergy are asexual. Cassocks are designed to mask a complete lack of libido. Ordination has the effect of erasing all knowledge of sex from the memory banks. 2) All clergy are sex-beasts engaged in three-in-a-bed romps with choristers and organist's wives. (This is helped on by the unfortunate coincidence that vicar rhymes with knicker.)

But it has to be said that the church has not enjoyed a happy reputation when it comes to sex. The belief that the flesh is inherently sinful and corrupt lingers on. I was amused to read a while ago that Orthodox Judaism has problems in this area, too. Rabbi Shmuley Boteach's book *Kosher Sex* caused shock waves. I'm not clear whether these shock waves rocked the synagogue, or just the journalistic community. He argues that Judaism "encourages sex for pleasure"; perhaps referring to the *Song of Songs*?—which is, of course, a wonderful piece of erotic verse, but I'm not sure it translates readily into manual-speke. A diagram of the female body helpfully labelled "heap of wheat" and "flock of goats moving down the slopes of Gilead" might leave many readers mystified.

These are a few of my least favourite things

Badly fitting bras

There has been quite a bit about bras in the papers recently. First there was that revolutionary new bra. I never bothered to find out what was so special about it, actually. Made of teflon with uplift powered by rocket fuel; or by some kind of green renewable energy source, more likely, that won't cause sparrows to disappear or the river Ouse to appear in people's sitting rooms. Whatever they were made out of they sounded jolly uncomfortable. I certainly haven't noticed an upsurge of pert profiles on the street. Then again, I wouldn't.

Then came the backlash suggestion that we might be better off without bras. This was the conclusion of a piece of research into sufferers from breast pain. Participants went bra-less for a few months and felt a whole lot better for it. Well, good for them. But if you are over a certain age and have fed numerous babies, I can't help feeling the Dimmock option is less viable. I discussed it with a friend and she hissed knowingly, "Spaniel's ears".

Anyway, the whole thing predictably got taken up by the media and given a new and terrifying spin: bras give you breast cancer. Later this was retracted. One thing is obvious, though—badly fitting bras are a pain and you're better off without them. But—ah, but!—a properly fitting bra can transform your life. And so I say to you, if you only do one thing this autumn, throw out your clapped-out old grey bras and get yourself measured properly. You may never appear to have four breasts under your T-shirt again!

Obviously, that piece of advice is aimed more at my female readers. My equivalent advice for men—unless you have already followed my suggestion for St Cosmas and Damian's Day—is get yourself off to a proper hair salon just for once and see what a difference it makes to break the £20 barrier. (Or the £40 barrier, if you live in London.) Spending £3 at Stavros' buzz-and-go barber's (even with a choice of free lecture on Cyprus or the Orthodox tradition thrown in) is not the same as a proper cut and blow dry. At salons you

"Let's see, dear; 40°C, low spin,
Caution: pressurized container, do not use near naked flame."

get to read *Hello* magazine and are served a cup of coffee into which hairclippings fall. *And* you get a free mint from the little bowl on the counter as you leave. Go on, try it. You may never drape again.

Saint of the week

LULL (8TH C), ARCHBISHOP OF MAINZ. FEAST: 16 OCTOBER.

EIGHTEENTH SUNDAY AFTER PENTECOST

or

THE SEVENTEENTH SUNDAY AFTER TRINITY

or

PENTECOST 18
(Trinity 17)
[Proper 19]
(Sludge green)

One of the joys of family holidays is Going for a Walk. If there is a large group of you this can require complex logistics to arrange. Almost as complex as doing tea and coffee after the meal. We spent half term in a large converted barn in Shropshire with the clan (my in-laws), and out of ten or so adults there were no two orders the same. It was like a flashback to making coffee for church meetings—tea, decaffeinated tea, Earl Grey, decaffeinated Earl Grey, coffee, decaffeinated coffee, full-fat milk, semi-skimmed milk, skimmed milk, black, organic semi-skimmed milk. In the end it seemed simpler to serve everyone mugs of hot water and let them put in their own additives.

Organizing the family ramble was a doddle after that. My contribution was to sit in another room reading a thriller while other people sorted it out, thereby reducing the number of cooks spoiling the broth by one. After much consulting of maps and books called things like *Two Hundred Country Rambles* (pub. 1978 before half the housing estates were built), *Across Shropshire with Gumboots and a Machete*, and *The Complete Guide to Getting Hopelessly Lost in Shropshire* and (most importantly of all) pub guides, a walk was decided on. We then debated which of our number could manage six miles and who, on grounds of old age, infirmity, extreme youth, poor walking boots and having a good thriller to finish, should be allowed to do a shorter stroll. Then we needed to establish how many cars were needed, who should be allowed to sit next to which cousin, how many hats, coats, children, boots, and Kit-kats to put in each car, but at last we were off.

My younger son hates walking, so he came with the silly shoe and arthritic-knee brigade. After a while he realized that he wasn't just looking at the view but was actually being taken on a walk and then he got grumpier and grumpier. The adults took it in turns to jolly him along by pointing out interesting pine-cones, but to no avail. He perked up no end when we hit a muddy patch, saying, "Oops!" in his innocent way. "Looks like we should have brought some spare clothes, Mum." Then the rest of us got grumpier and grumpier as we sploshed and waded our way along, cursing inconsiderate horseriders for churning up the path.

My older son went with the big boys. This was something of a breakthrough, as three years ago he swore blind he was never going on one of Grandpa's walks ever again. This time, when asked if he was enjoying it, he replied, "Yes. It releases a lot of stress and gives me a great sense of achievement." So there you are. Next time life gets on top of you, go and climb a steep hill.

Bad mother award

I have to confess that there are times when my children call me to sing them a bedtime song and I find myself grinding my teeth and snarling, rather than scampering dewy-eyed to tuck them up. It's something to do with being summoned by the bellow "Mu-u-um!" If I ignore it the volume goes up a notch with each successive roar, so to spare the ears of the PCC officers meeting below, or whatever, I go and sing. My older son usually wants "Cheer up, ye saints of God, there's nothing to worry about!", a chorus from my nonconformist childhood which fails, quite startlingly, to take into account global warming, Foot and Mouth, BSE, AIDS and cellulite.

On one occasion he told me he wanted "As the deer plants for the water." "You mean 'As the deer *pants* for the water'," I corrected.

"No I don't!" he said, wearing his "You can't fool me, Mum" expression. "How come everyone else in my school says 'plants'?" "Everyone else is wrong," I replied. "Hasn't it ever occurred to you, Mum, that *you* might be wrong, just for once?" I spent five minutes arguing my case, but he remains unconvinced that any hymn they sing at school could possibly contain the word "pants".

Saint of the week

ETHBIN (6TH C), MONK AND HERMIT. FEAST: 19 OCTOBER.

NINETEENTH SUNDAY AFTER PENTECOST

or

THE EIGHTEENTH SUNDAY AFTER TRINITY

or

PENTECOST 19
(Trinity 18)
[Proper 20]
(Snot green)

========

Another Hallowe'en is almost upon us. One of our local papers has very helpfully provided its readers with a large sign bearing a crossed-out pumpkin and the words "Sorry—no trick or treat." All I have to do is scribble out the word "sorry" and write "Push off" over the top and stick it up in the porch. I hope somebody will be producing another one for Christmas which reads "Bah! Humbug! No pathetic out-of-tune carols".

I must confess, I wouldn't have dared put up a sign like that when we lived in Gateshead. I just handed over the sweets for fear of reprisals. Compromising one's principles seemed the only rational response to the possibility of a brick through the window. The doorbell was rung non-stop all evening by kids in feeble bin-bag cloaks uttering the traditional elevated verse associated with Hallowe'en: "Trick or treat, Smell my feet, give me something nice to eat." There are several possible responses, like "On your bike, you little tyke, before I prod you with this spike." I try to reclaim All Hallow's Eve by carving pumpkins with crosses or fishes on, but I'd rather ban the whole thing. Kids out raking the street at all hours, old people frightened in their homes. Terrible.

And anyway, why celebrate evil? Why back the loser? But maybe it's just a vanity thing. You somehow know you're going to look thinner dressed as a witch than as an angel. The slimming effects of wearing black defy theology, I'm afraid.

But why should the devil have all the good costumes? You're invited to an All Saints party—how to look glamorous? Don't just come as you are in honour of St Michael. Much too obvious. Homobonus is the patron saint of tailors. Crispin and Crispinian are patrons of leatherworkers—scope there for the imaginative, I feel. Basically, you pick your favourite dressing-up gear and look up your patron saint (WWI flying ace—Joseph of Copertino; go-go dancer—St Vitus). Or you could approach it from the emblem angle. Who am I? Eyes (on dish)—Lucy. Intestines—Erasmus. Boys in tub—Nicholas. Head held in hands—Denys, Oswald, Sidwell, Sigfrid, etc.

I love All Saints day with its annual reminder that we are part of something vast. I can remember the time when the concept of the communion of saints spring to life for me. It was the day my grandfather died. I was in church saying the words we say at every communion: "With angels and archangels *and all the company of heaven....*" Frankly, pumpkins just don't compete.

Saint of the week

ERC (DATE UNKNOWN), BISHOP (?). PATRON OF ST ERTH, CORNWALL.
FEAST: 31 OCTOBER.

TWENTIETH SUNDAY AFTER PENTECOST

or

THE NINETEENTH SUNDAY AFTER TRINITY

or

PENTECOST 20
(Trinity 19)
[Proper 21]
(Any olivacious, virescent shade)

———————

Hallowe'en gets its fair share of condemnation, but I'm surprised how few Christians are bothered by Bonfire Night. Burning Roman Catholics in effigy? What kind of a witness is that? Half the kids who go around wanting a penny for the guy haven't a clue about the real significance of what they're doing. For a start they're out begging any time after the beginning of October. *When* is Guy Fawkes night, children? I want to enquire in schoolmarmy tones. And another thing—that's not a guy, that's a teddy bear in a Newcastle United away strip! You're not going to burn it, are you? So it's not a guy, is it? So no penny. Someone told me they once saw some kids pushing their baby brother in a buggy and wanting a penny for the guy.

The traditional reason for wanting pennies is to spend them on fireworks, of course. Kids have been throwing bangers around here for weeks already. Today I saw a new refinement—put the firework in a bottle and make the bottle explode! Much more exciting. Kids are very inventive when it comes to new forms of mischief, and putting explosives within their reach is simply asking for trouble.

I'd like to see the sale of fireworks to the public banned. For every happy back-garden display there are dozens of kids running horrible risks and dozens of victims of pranks. And from what I remember of the average box of fireworks, it's pretty tame stuff compared with proper public displays. "This one's called 'golden fleece'," Dad shouts. Lights blue touchpaper and retires. Long pause. Pathetic *whoosh*! followed by sprinkle sprinkle and Mum going, "Ooh, isn't that pretty, girls?" and us thinking, "Was that *it*?"

After the tragic accidents a few years ago involving powerful fireworks with instructions (helpfully!) in Chinese, I think the time has come to say goodbye to amateur displays.

These are a few of my least favourite things

Drunkenness

The area round our church has recently been gentrified. The whole place looks a lot more respectable. This is during the day, however. All the refurbished buildings seem to be reopening as wine bars to complement the two pubs already within spitting distance of the church. Peeing distance would be a more accurate description, perhaps. The church wall seems to double as a urinal on Friday and Saturday nights when the street turns into puke city as the bar and pub customers engage in the local pastimes of violent affray, kicking the church windows in and vomit-skating.

"*Sadly, it's not my Charismatic preaching— it's the influence of another spirit.*"

Walsall is not the only place to have fallen victim to what looks like foolhardy town-centre planning. A study undertaken at Durham University a while back has painted a bleak picture of modern drinking habits. Large numbers of late-licence bars and clubs clustered in a single street has driven violent crime up in many areas. Town planners trying to create a balance of different types of club find their work is undermined by breweries wanting to sell as much as possible as fast as possible at the greatest profit.

Handy hints from the vicar's wife

How to deter drunks from peeing against the church

Why not run mains electricity through a wire along the church wall?

Saint of the week

BIRSTAN (10TH C), BISHOP OF WINCHESTER. FEAST: 4 NOVEMBER.

TWENTY-FIRST SUNDAY AFTER PENTECOST

or

THE TWENTIETH SUNDAY AFTER TRINITY

or

PENTECOST 21

or

THE LAST SUNDAY AFTER TRINITY

(Trinity 20)

[Proper 22]

(Oh, wear what you like. I don't care.)

=====

This Remembrance Sunday our congregation took part in the service at the cenotaph, rather than holding our own act of remembrance during the service and having the strains of "Hello, hello, whose your lady friend?" from the retreating band outside cutting across the Eucharistic prayer.

Here in the clement Midlands it was a crisp sunny day, and not a cloud in the sky. Having arrived a little late we were some way from the main action and the children couldn't really see what was going on. After a few minutes mine started muttering, "This is really boring. When can we go back to church?" The bright spot was the gun being fired. My younger son looked round eagerly and asked, "Are they shooting the pigeons?" If only they were. I'm afraid the sermon and prayers passed the children by. They rallied a little as a breeze picked up and began making (to the six and nine-year-old mind) "rude yet amusing" noises with the microphone. I was reluctant to be too strict with them as most of the people around us seemed to be chatting throughout anyway. One man was smoking next to me and there was a distinct whiff of pub in the air. I wondered why they were all there. If it was a mark of respect then it wasn't a very vigorous one. Perhaps going to the Remembrance Sunday parade is simply one of the "done" things, like buying an Advent calendar.

My attitude to Remembrance Day has changed over the years. As a child I could make little of it, possibly because nobody in my immediate family was killed in either war, and those with bad experiences tended not to speak of them. It wasn't until a few weeks ago when my younger son had a piece of homework which involved asking relatives about their memories of the war that I found out about what it had been like for my father living in Kent as a child during the Second World War.

As a young adult wrestling with pacifism, I had reservations about big parades and worries about jingoism, but in recent years— since having sons, in fact—I have been able to glimpse what the sacrifice of so many people must have been like. A few weeks ago I was in a churchyard in a little hamlet and read a plaque on one wall of the lychgate. It was dedicated by a widow to her husband and "to all the other dear lads in the choir and congregation". I turned and looked on the opposite wall and there were eighteen names. Eighteen men from one small community. How can we not reflect on what a terrible thing war is? Watching my children messing about and giggling in the November sun I was reassured that this is, in part, what the sacrifice was about—that future generations of children should be free to be children: fooling around, carefree and without a clue about what war is like.

These are a few of my least favourite things

Hanging about at airports

I spent rather a lot of time—and even more money—in Birmingham airport last Saturday. I was collecting a Revolutionary Communist I know who was visiting from Geneva. We found the arrivals lounge and saw an ominous little sign saying "cancelled". I found out later from my friend that there were only five passengers so they just called the whole thing off and sent everyone to Brussels instead. (Is this an idea that will transfer to 8 o'clock BCP Holy Communion, I wonder? Just a thought.) I was then faced with a dilemma. Which would be worse: driving all the way home then driving back an hour later, or staying in the airport with two children for two-and-a-half hours? I asked the children what they thought, and they, shrewdly assessing the situation's potential for bubble gum, coke, croissants, Thornton's chocolate and Pokemon comics, opted to stay put. Let me tell you, the Visa card had to go home and have a little lie down in a darkened room after *that* morning's work.

I noticed that one of the coffee outlets went under the motto "coffee for life", which despite the vast outlay of the morning's trip, must still work out as a net saving. One cappuccino there and I'd never have to buy another for the entire rest of my existence. I was even more struck by the words inscribed on the inside rim of the cup: "Coffee is life". A slightly bold soteriological claim for a hot beverage, I felt.

Saint of the week

ABBO (11TH C), ABBOT. FEAST: 13 NOVEMBER.

EPILOGUE

Here we are, at the end of another church year. It feels odd, doesn't it, to break off for no apparent reason in November? But we are odd here on Planet Anglicanism. We persist in doing things our way, even if nobody else does them like that. We believe in things normal people find ludicrous, like the virgin birth, the resurrection and letting grown men dress in curtain material and pointy hats, while still expecting them to be taken seriously.

So back we go to Stir-up Sunday and the whole process begins all over again. The passage of time is grim, relentlessly linear and "like an ever-rolling stream bears all its sons away". But the revolving church year gives some rhythm to our lives, provides us with a sense of times and seasons, gives us a context for "the trivial round, the common task" which might otherwise grind us down. It also allows us to feel part of something grander, and who knows, now and then we might even catch an echo of eternity.

"Sorry we're a bit late this year, luv—we've been experiencing delays due to the wrong kind of guy."

GLOSSARY

A

Advent	season before Christmas
All-age Worship	service for young children
Alpha Course	famous introduction-to-Christianity course instrumental in bringing many thousands to faith, but exercising a policy of refusing permission to churches wanting to adapt material for local needs
altar	incorrect term for holy table
altar cloth	incorrect term for holy tablecloth
Alternative Episcopal Oversight	Anglican equivalent of taking your ball home
Alternative Service Book	obsolete (and little mourned) service book
anchoress	pious (medieval) female bricked up in church wall
Anglicanism	the art of being an Anglican
Anglo-Catholic	High Church Anglican
archbishop	most senior Anglican management figure
archdeacon	priest, Anglican middle management figure
ASB	Alternative Service Book, *see above*
Ascension Day	festival celebrating our Lord's ascension. Thursday, forty days after resurrection
Ash Wednesday	first day of Lent
Anglican	of the Church of England—but only in UK

B

baptism	Christian initiation rite
bazaar	indoor means of fund-raising by selling cakes and gonks
BCP	Book of Common Prayer, *see below*
biretta	small handgun sported by Roman (and some Anglo-) Catholic priests
bishop	senior Anglican management figure, top ranking officer
Book of Common Prayer	very redundant service book, but with beautiful language
BVM	Blessed Virgin Mary

C

C of E	Church of England
cassock	long black frock worn by clergy
cassock alb	Ku Klux Klan outfit worn by liberal Catholics
catholic	universal
Catholic (Anglo-)	High Church Anglican
Catholic (liberal)	pertaining to form of Anglo-Catholicism brought up to date and made relevant to the 1960s

Catholic (Roman)	Roman Catholic
charge (Archdeacon's)	rallying cry to new churchwardens
choir	group of singers in robes
chorus	worship song
christening	infant baptism
clergy	ordained person
clerical shirt	shirt worn by ordained person
collation	ceremony in which new archdeacon is collated
communion	the Lord's Supper
compline	night time service
consecrate	to lead communion service, or make a bishop
cope	bishop's poncho
crozier	bishop's crook
curate	trainee vicar
CW	Common Worship (new version of Book of Common Prayer)

D

deacon	most junior Anglican rank
deanery	small geographical area containing several parishes
deanery synod	group of people waiting to go home
diocese	large geographical area containing many parishes
dog collar	means of restraint for difficult clergy

E

Easter	the day Jesus rose from the dead
ecumenical	inter-church
elements	bread and wine at communion
Ember Day	the morning after the church burns down
Emmaus Course	Christian version of Alpha
Epiphany	Manifestation of Christ to the Gentiles
episcopal	relating to bishops
Eucharist	the Lord's Supper or Holy Communion
Evangelical	us
Evensong	evening service

F

fête	outdoor means of fund-raising by selling gonks and cakes
font	tiny baptistry or mixing bowl

G

genuflection	liturgical curtseying
Glasgow	place to which rail fare is required by callers at the vicarage

H

hassock	kneeler

High Church	Anglo-Catholic
homily	sermon lite

I

incumbent	priest (vicar) who cannot be moved on by bishop
intercessions	led prayers during a service
interregnum	job vacancy between vicars

J

Jesus	founder of Church

K

kneeler	hassock
knickers	useful rhyme with 'vicars'

L

Lady Chapel	High Church team for crèche area
laity	non-clergy people
lay person	non-clergy person
lectionary	book containing appointed Bible readings for services
Lent	season of self-denial before Easter
licensing	service to install new clergy person
liturgical	relating to liturgy
liturgy	form of public worship
locum	cheap holiday for clergy

M

Magi	the Wise Men
Manifestation of Christ to the Gentiles	Epiphany, arrival of Wise Men
Mass	the Lord's Supper, pron. "maaarss" in Anglo-Catholic circles
Matins	BCP morning service
Maundy Thursday	day before Good Friday
mitre	bishop's hat
Morning Prayer	morning service
Mothering Sunday	proper term for Mothers' Day
mozzetta	type of cheese
music group	group of unrobed musicians

N

nunc dimittis	beginning of prayer of Simeon, in Latin, used at Evening Worship

O

OHP	overhead projector
order	Anglican clergy rank, eg. deacon, priest, bishop

Ordinary Time	breathing space between church seasons
ordination	service to make candidates into clergy persons
overconsecrate	to bless too much bread and wine for communion

P

palm cross	small cross made out of palm branch
Palm Sunday	Sunday before Easter
parish	geographical area having own church and clergy
parishioner	person living in parish
Paschal candle	Easter candle
Passion Sunday	fifth Sunday in Lent
Passiontide	the fortnight before Easter
PCC	Parochial Church Council elected to thwart vicar
PCC officers	sub committee of PCC, typically churchwardens, treasurer, secretary
Pentecost	the day the Holy Spirit was poured out on the church
Petertide	time around St Peter's Day, often the time of ordinations
pew	indoor church bench
purificators	communion table napkins
priest	second rank clergy person
priest-in-charge	priest (vicar) who can be moved on by the bishop
proper	designated readings for worship

Q

Quinquagesima	Sunday before Lent
quinquennial	five-yearly inspection
quota	how much each parish has to pay to the Diocese

R

Refreshment Sunday	Sunday midway through Lent
reredos	fancy church screen
Resolutions A, B and C	Anglican legislation to authorise schism
Revised Common Lectionary	service book in current use
robinia	small brown red-breasted European bird (*Erithacus rubecola*); tassels traditionally attached to biretta
Rogationtide	I have no idea
Roman Catholic	our friends, the Papists

S

Sankey and Moody	proto Graham Kendricks
sexton	church official. Grave-digging a speciality
Stir-up Sunday	Sunday before Advent at which church gossip is exchanged
spiky	Anglo-Catholic
Shrove Tuesday	Pancake Day
Sexagesima	Sunday before Quinquagesima

swearing in	chance for new churchwardens to vent their feelings
sermon	heavyweight homily
Septuagesima	Sunday before Sexagesima
suffragan	assistant bishop
stock	backless clerical shirt with no sleeves
soutane	seedless raisin from small pale yellow grape, used in puddings and cakes
stole	past tense of steal
soteriological	relating to salvation

T

Tantrism	mystical branch of Hinduism/Buddhism
Transfiguration	festival celebrating Christ's transfiguration
theological college	place where clergy are trained
team vicar	vicar of group "team" of parishes
Trinity	central dogma of Christianity, viz. that the One God exists in Three Persons and One Substance.

U

underconsecrate	to bless insufficient bread and wine at communion
UPA	Urban Priority Area

V

vicar	job of being parish priest
vicarage	smallish modern house in grounds of Georgian former rectory
verger	church official who shows people to their seats
vestments	fancy clothes worn by clergy
Vespers	small motor scooters ridden by Italian priests
vigil	eve of a festival
visiting	clergy pastime

W

Whitsuntide	proper term of Pentecost
wafer	communion bread substitute

X

Xmas	Christmas